jamboree

~ COMMUNICATION ~
ACTIVITIES FOR CHILDREN

John Palim and Paul Power

Nelson

Nelson English Language Teaching
100 Avenue Road
London NW3 3HF

An International Thomson Publishing Company

London • Bonn • Boston • Madrid • Melbourne • Mexico City •
New York • Paris • Singapore • Tokyo

© John Palim and Paul Power 1990

First published by Nelson ELT 1990

ISBN 0-17-555895-7
NPN 9 8 7 6 5 4

Printed in China

Acknowledgements

Our grateful thanks are due to

ITS English School, Hastings, for the use of their word processing and other facilities;

Jane Pettigrew and Geoffrey Tyler for permission to reproduce the words and music for
the songs in activities G6, G7, and G8, – these songs first appeared in the
Montessori publication *Early Start with Language and Song*;

Phyllis Vannuffel for ideas for activities and visuals;

Diane Hall and Kate Robinson of Thomas Nelson for their ideas and encouragement;

and not least Sebastian Power, Seeta Palim and Shanta Palim for contributing and trying
out a number of the activities.

The publishers would also like to thank John Green of Tadpole Books for providing the
artwork for the above-mentioned songs.

Contents

Section E – Writing Activities

Section F – Discovery Activities

Making Sense of Things

Section G – Songs, Rhymes and Chants

Section H – Games, Puzzles and Quizzes

Photocopiable pages

Introduction

The book and its purpose

The book is a resource book for teachers of children aged six to eleven years old who are learning English. It is a supplementary book providing extra language practice through educationally sound activities.

It is provided for teachers to dip into when they feel the need to enhance and reinforce the normal teaching syllabus, and is not intended to be worked through activity by activity or to be used for presenting language for the first time. It is not a coursebook.

Although many language activities at this age should be game-like to maintain the children's interest, the book is not simply a collection of games. Somes games are included, but these, like the other activities, have a specific language purpose.

The book contains over 100 stimulating and enjoyable activities which promote the learning of English and encourage children to communicate. These cover the four language skills and many of the language points learners need at this age. The eight activity types are those which teachers find useful in developing language abilities in children:

A	Colouring and drawing	**E**	Writing activities
B	Making things	**F**	Discovery activities
C	Games with movement	**G**	Songs, rhymes and chants
D	Stories and speaking activities	**H**	Quizzes, games and puzzles

At the end is a section of 26 pages (A–Z) of illustrations which teachers can freely photocopy. Many of the activities make use of these pages, but you will find many other uses for them.

How to use the activities

- You can use some activities as complete lessons in themselves.
- You can integrate many activities into your syllabus. Look at the index to find the language focus you wish to practise. Look through the activities sections to find the type of activity you want the children to do.
- You can use shorter activities to fill in the odd 10 or 15 minutes.
- You can use any of the activities for revision.

- **Preparation:** Many of the activities require no preparation at all. For many others you only need to collect the materials required or photocopy a page in the photocopiable section. Look below the language box to see if any preparation is needed.

- Many activities have extensions, adaptations and alternative versions:
  an **alternative** is a **different way** of doing the main activity. It has the same language focus.
  an **extension leads on** from the main activity.
  an **adaptation** can be used **instead of,** or **as well as,** the main activity. It often has a different language focus or is for a different age group.

At the page edge you will see symbols which indicate
- the **age** which the activity is suitable for, such as

  This does not relate to the language level — it is based on the age by which children should be capable of dealing with the concept. Some classes will be able to cope with the language and some will not. Look at the language box and decide if your class can cope with the language, or if you can simplify it using language they know.
- **length of time** needed for the activity

| 5–10 minute filler | part of a lesson | 30 minutes or more | whole lesson | more than 1 lesson |

However, the time taken will vary with the age and level of the class.

- **materials** required, for example

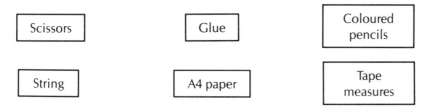

| Scissors | Glue | Coloured pencils |
| String | A4 paper | Tape measures |

A4 is used here, but other similar sizes of paper are acceptable. We assume all children have a notebook, pencil, rubber and ruler. 'Sticky tack' refers to products such as 'Blu-tak' or 'Buddies', used for sticking paper or card onto a wall or board but which can easily be removed.

- **classroom organisation and student interaction**

children work individually **IW**   children work as a class, or teacher to class interaction **CW**

children work in pairs **PW**

children work in two or more teams **TW**

children work in small groups **GW**

Most of the activities in the book require children to work in pairs or small groups. This gives children the maximum opportunity to speak, and speaking is the most natural means of communicating, especially for children. When a child has to speak in front of the whole class, he or she often feels inhibited. The others become impatient waiting for their turn. Besides, children prefer to communicate with their friends rather than with teachers.

- Below the title of each activity you will see a **language box.** This gives the main language areas the children will practise. These may be:

functions   vocabulary   spelling

structures   pronunciation

Make sure children already know these areas. As a general rule, don't use the activities to introduce new language, though you can pre-teach any specific vocabulary needed. You should not expect to find all the language specified in detail. Indeed, you should encourage children to use as much other language as possible, and adapt to your particular classes the basic language given in *italics*.

Much of the value of these activities is in the incidental language which children have to use:

What's _____ in English?　　　*It's your turn.*
That's wrong, it should be red.　　*I don't understand.*
What do we do next?　　　　　*I've forgotten what to do next.*
Is this right?　　　　　　　　*Can I have some more paper?*
I'll draw this again.　　　　　*Pardon?*

You can teach these formally to the children, or informally to a few children at a time when you find they are using their mother tongue instead of English.

- To the right hand side of the language box you will see the **main skill** to be practised. Nearly all activities involve other skills beside the main one.

L　　　　**S**　　　　**R**　　　　**W**

listening　　　speaking　　　reading　　　writing

- An asterisk * indicates that the step is optional; it is probably better to do with older or more confident children.

- Language used by the teacher which the children need to understand but not say is given in italics as follows: *teacher's language.*

- Language which the children need to use is given in bold italics as follows: ***children's language.***

- Within each section, the activities are arranged in approximately the chronological order in which a child would be able to do the activities. This is based partly on the language level and partly on the ability of the child to cope with the concept at the lower age limit specified.

- For convenience the teacher is referred to throughout as 'she' and the children or child as 'he'. When several children are involved they are referred to as **C1, C2** etc. (child 1, child 2).

- L1 refers to the children's first language, sometimes used to discuss points of English.

About teaching children

Children are not adults. They are still learning about the world. They are learning a sense of space and time. It is no use asking a six-year-old child to imagine what it was like living 1000 years ago, or to imagine travelling to Africa.

They are learning to classify things and relate things to each other. A seven-year-old child is still learning that a cup is like a bottle because they can both contain liquids.

It is only near the top of this age range that children are becoming capable of abstract thought. All children achieve these stages, but at different ages. You may well find some children can do things which other children cannot. These differences are not due to lack of ability but to a different rate of development. Therefore it is all the more necessary to treat children as individuals. You must make your own judgements about whether a particular activity is suitable for **your** children.

Don't expect children to do things in English before they have learned to do them in their own language — things like telling the time, or being able to read and write.

However, children have a great capacity for acquiring language through exposure to language, e.g., looking and listening, as well as through formal teaching. Your job is to provide opportunities for both. You can use a small amount of language which you haven't systematically taught. The children will acquire the meaning through your repetition and the context you use it in, for example:
Well done. I like the way you've drawn that.

Children learn by **doing.** They learn through using their senses more than adults do. They will enjoy role play more if they can dress up for it and use real things. They learn language by **using** it — listening to it, speaking it, reading it, writing it.

Children learn best when they are **motivated**
— by being interested in the activity
— by seeing an end result which gives them a feeling of achievement (so display their work!)
— by being involved in activities which are relevant to them (so use their interests, experiences, background and environment).

Children are easily discouraged and lose interest if the task is too difficult. Ensure that the tasks you set are **within their ability.**

Some dos and don'ts

- Don't think of children in terms of levels. They may not acquire a mastery of structures as systematically as adults.

- Set your 'class rules' from the first day. It is easier to be firm at first and then relax, than tighten discipline later. Create a good working relationship with each child individually. Do this by setting up a caring yet secure environment. The motto is: **Be firm, fair and friendly.**

- Start learning the children's names from the first day. Fold a piece of paper with the name written in large letters and place it on the desk or floor in front of each child.

- Don't be afraid to let children talk. Use the things they want to talk about and the ideas they want to express as a medium for learning.

- Give clear instructions. If children are not sure what to do, the lesson will fail. Teach simple instructions that you will use regularly: *Ready, Steady, Go.*
  Hands up those who _____ .
  Children in team A are _____ .
  Also try to use English even when you don't have to, e.g. for general administration:
  Can you open the window a little more?
  Go to the office and ask for some coloured chalk.
  This is **real** communication.

- Use the mother tongue to give instructions if they are very complex. But remember that children can often understand instructions even when the language is more difficult than anything they have learned. It is very important for children to have the experience of responding to these instructions given in English. This is how they will learn to understand normal English speech. Of course you can use gesture and mime to help them understand.
- Encourage children to use English as much as possible. They will revert to the mother tongue if they are bored or uncertain what to do.
- Encourage children to listen to and read English wherever possible. Sources include TV programmes and cartoons, notices, labels and English comics. These display **authentic** English.
- Don't always expect a spoken response. Children can indicate comprehension by a gesture or by carrying out an instruction. Don't rush children into speaking before they are ready or you may take away the confidence which they are building up.
- Draw where possible on what children are studying in other classes and the mainstream curriculum. Integrate other subjects into your lessons where possible. You will find examples of this in the book.
- Have a resource box. Children can contribute empty boxes, jars, yogurt pots, old toys (make sure they are safe and not broken), buttons, clothes for dressing up.
- Children have a short concentration span. Change the activity to ensure children remain interested. Don't continue to the bitter end just because **you** feel there is more to be got from it. Judge the mood of the class. When they lose concentration, they stop learning.
- Children are still learning to work with others. Some will be leaders and some followers. You may need to organise your groups so that children work together effectively.
- Don't be afraid to let children move about. Change your classroom seating arrangements if you are able to. Try not to have children sitting behind rows of desks. To communicate, children need to face each other. Have a system where children can move into pairs and groups without a lot of fuss and bother. If children are in rows and you are not allowed to change this, at least have them sitting in pairs. For group work you simply ask alternate rows to turn their chairs round.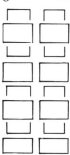
- Vary pairs and groups so that children don't always work with best friends. You can do many pair and group activities more than once by changing round the pairs and groups.
- When children are working in pairs and groups, don't just sit and watch. Go round the class helping the weaker children, prompting others, checking language and monitoring the progress of the activity.
- Continually check that children actually **are** doing what you have set them to do. When speaking to the whole class, make sure all the children are quiet and listening to you. You should not have to raise your voice. Provide plenty of repetition. Children do not always listen even when they seem to.
- Try to get children using the short forms **'s, 'll, n't** etc. in speech, as this is essential for English rhythm. This is easier if you get them into the habit from the start, so use them yourself.
- Correct children's pronunciation, but don't let your correction interfere with communication, or disrupt the activity. It is not necessary to correct **every** mistake.
- Write neatly using clear print. With older children you can start to use clear joined up writing.
- When children finish a piece of work, make sure you acknowledge it, and praise it where appropriate. Children respond to praise and encouragement so give this freely. They do not respond to sarcasm and excessive criticism.
- Remember that children are establishing their abilities to build personal relationships all the time they are growing. Your attitude to them is crucial as it will affect their whole view of the world as well as of language and of learning.
- Communicate with parents whenever possible. Tell them what you are doing in your lessons and why.
- Make learning English a joyful activity, to develop a positive attitude to language learning.
- **Don't forget you are teachers of children, not just teachers of English.**

Section A Colouring and drawing

A1 Picture Squares

Practising numbers 1–10 and letters A-J	L

6+

Coloured pencils

X

IW

Preparation

Make copies of page **X**, so that each child has a 10 x 10 box square. Write letters A-J across the top and nos 1–10 down the side of each box.

Steps

1   Give each child a box square. Tell them you are going to call out a number and a letter. When they hear the letter they should look along the top of the box square and when they hear the number they should look down the side. They find the square where the two rows meet. You may have to demonstrate this once or twice until they get the idea.
2   When they have found the square they should colour it in. They can choose the colour themselves or you can extend the activity by giving the colour:
    Example   *Colour B3 blue.*
3   Call out the numbers and letters in turn as below.
4   Finally, get the children to compare their pictures in pairs and with yours and ask them what they think the picture is.

Extension A1a

To practise other letters and numbers, you can change the references to 11–20, K-T etc.
Here are the references for building up three pictures. You can easily devise more pictures by using the blank box squares, and older children can make up their own pictures to try out on their partners. Remember that not all objects can be built up from squares; an apple built up from squares may not resemble an apple.

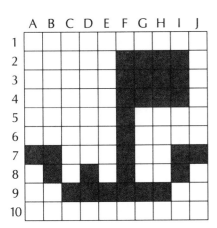
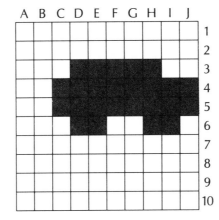
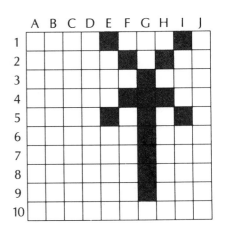

SHIP   A7 B7 B8 C9 D8 D9 E9 F2 F3 F4 F5 F6 F7 F8 F9 G2 G3 G4 G9 H2 H3 H4 H9 I2 I3 I4 I7 I8 J7

CAR   C4 C5 D3 D4 D5 D6 E3 E4 E5 E6 F3 F4 F5 G3 G4 G5 H3 H4 H5 H6 I4 I5 I6 J4 J5

WINDMILL   E1 E5 F2 F4 G3 G4 G5 G6 G7 G8 G9 H2 H4 I1 I5

A2 Join the Dots

Practising numbers 1–40	L

J

PW

Preparation

Make copies of page **J**, one for each pair.

Steps

1   Put the children into pairs. Cut the copies in two and give C1 to child **1** and C2 to child **2.**
2   C1 now calls out the numbers on his sheet while C2 ioins up the dots to form a picture. C2 then does the same by calling out his numbers while C1 joins the dots.
3   When most of the class have finished, ask them what they can see in their picture (a mouse or an owl/a bird).

A3 Labelling Clothes

Practising clothes vocabulary	W

Scissors, glue, coloured pencils

C

IW

Preparation

Make copies of page **C**, 1 for each child.

Steps

1   Ask the children for names of clothes and write them on the board.
2   Write some new items which they do not know and illustrate with the real thing or draw a simple picture on the board. Practise the pronunciation.
3   Give each child some or all of the pictures from page **C**. They should cut these out and put the pictures in one pile and the words in another.
4   They should colour and stick the pictures in their books, then either match and stick the words or label their drawings. (They should write *a shirt* rather than just *shirt*). Rub out the drawings on the board while they are cutting.
*   Faster learners could draw and label pictures of other clothes items, or write a sentence:
    Example   *I wear a white shirt at school. We wear gloves when it is cold.*

Adaptation A3a Clothes Matching Game

Practising clothes vocabulary ***Have you got _____ ?*** ***No, I haven't/Yes, I have***	S

GW

Steps

1 and **2** as before.
3   Put the children in groups of 3. Give each group 1 copy of page **C**. When they have cut out the words and pictures each child takes 6 pictures of clothes.
4   They should put the words face down in a pile on the table. Each child in turn picks up a word and asks another child by name, ***Pierre, have you got a shirt?*** for example.
5   If Pierre has the correct picture he gives it to the first child, who puts it with the correct word in front of him, or sticks it in his book. If not, the word goes to the bottom of the pile. Children ask only one question in turn. The child with most pairs of pictures and words wins.

Alternative A3b Memory game

Steps

1　Put the children in groups of 3 or 4.
　　Cut out the clothes and the word labels, and place all the pictures and words face down.

2　The children take it in turns to turn over 1 picture and 1 word. As they turn each one over they should say the name of the item in the picture, and read the word on the label. If they are the same then the child can keep the pair and have another turn.

3　If the picture and word do not match, the child must turn them face down again in the same place. The next child has a turn. When all the papers have been taken, the child with the most pairs wins.

A4　Match the Teacher's Drawing

| Developing listening for detail Clothes and colours *_____ has (got) white socks and black shoes* | L | 6–9 |

Scissors, glue, coloured pencils

C, P

PW

Preparation

Prepare 1 copy of page **C** and 1 of **P**. Prepare 4 large clothed figures, each wearing different clothes of different colours, and give each one a name.
Make copies of **P**, 1 between 8 children, so that each pair has 1 large figure, and copies of **C**, 1 for each pair.

Steps

1　Give 1 figure to each pair and tell them the name of the figure they have.
　　Give 1 copy of page **C** and tell them to cut out the clothes.

2　Describe what your figures are wearing without letting the children see them:
　　Example　*Mario has white socks and black shoes, but Paola has yellow socks and brown shoes.*
　　　　　　Antonio's shirt is blue, but Mario's is green . . .
　　Suit the language to the ability of the class. The children must colour the clothes for their own figure. Repeat the descriptions several times, as necessary.

3　Tell the children to stick the clothes on their figure. Ask to see all the 'Mario's' and show yours.
　　Children comment on any differences:
　　Example　**My Mario has got black shoes, but your Mario has got brown shoes.**
　　Repeat with the other figures.

Alternative A4a

Do not use page **C**. Prepare figures by drawing in and colouring the clothes on **P** on your figures and asking the children to draw on and colour clothes to match your description.

A5　Washing Line

| Developing listening comprehension Clothes and colours Prepositions: *in the middle, on the right/left, between* | L | 6–10 |

A4 paper, coloured pencils

IW

Steps

1　Tell children they are going to help to hang out the washing.
　　Tell them to draw a line across their sheet of paper.

2　Tell children: *Hang a red sweater in the middle.*
　　Children draw and colour accordingly.
　　Then *Hang a pair of yellow socks on the left.*
　　　　Hang a blue shirt between the socks and the sweater etc.
　　Children compare with each other and point out differences.

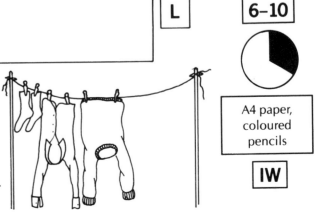

Note: Before starting, demonstrate on the board, for example, showing that you mean on the right side of the washing line, not right of the red sweater.

Alternative A5a

Make copies of page **C**, 1 for each group of 3 or 4.
Use cutouts on page **C**. In groups, children stick these onto a large sheet of paper or, using paper clips or clothes pegs, a piece of string tied between two chairs.

A6 Is Your House Like Mine?

> Practising prepositions and adverbs of place
> Vocabulary: rooms and furniture
> * *is/isn't like* _____

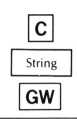

Preparation

Make a copy of pages **H** and **F**. Cut out and stick furniture in the house. Add windows if you like. This is the teacher's house. Make enough copies of **H** and **F** for 1 of each between 2.
Practise the necessary language: *in/near/by/between/in front of/behind/on the left/on the right; upstairs/downstairs; living room/dining room/hall/kitchen/bedroom/bathroom.*

Steps

1   Give a copy of pages **H** and **F** to each pair. Tell them to cut out the furniture. Quicker learners can help the slower ones.
2   Explain that you are going to describe your house and they are going to make a house like yours. They can't see your house so they have to listen to you and put the furniture in the right place.
3   Describe your house room by room repeating the descriptions several times:
Example   *I've got a table in the living room. It's by the window.* With more advanced pupils you can use more complex sentences:
Example   *Upstairs in the first bedroom near the stairs there are two beds.*
If children ask for more details, like **Which side?** (If they ask in their mother tongue, repeat the question in English) you can give them, for example, *On the left. Near the door.*
4   Ask to see the houses and show yours. Children comment on any differences.
Children go round to other desks looking at other houses, spotting the number of differences.
Point out that differences are not necessarily wrong:
Example   *I said the table is by the window, so you are right.*
        That's OK. I didn't say if it is this side or this side (pointing), *so both are right.*
*As they visit other pairs children can say, for example, **Your bedroom is like the teacher's** or
Our living room isn't like Miss Day's (because we put the table here).

Note: Younger children will only be able to cope with one or two items in each room.

Extension A6a

> Understanding descriptions
> Colours, rooms and furniture

Coloured pencils

This activity can be done later, or for homework.

Preparation
*Write out and photocopy a description as below.

Steps
1   Children copy from the board, or you can give them a photocopied description:
Example   *My kitchen floor is green and yellow. My bath and toilet are pink . . .*
2   Children colour in their houses from activity **A6**, following the description.

Note: This can also be done with the teacher describing orally.

A7 Moving Pictures

Practising present continuous for present action
> ***What's the dog doing?***
> ***It's running***

A4 paper, scissors

IW

Steps

1   Give each child a sheet of A4 paper, or 1 sheet between 2 if they are going to do 2, not 4, drawings. They should cut it into 4 strips about 7.5 cm wide, across the short side. While they are doing this, draw one pair of the drawings below on the board.

2   Children fold one strip in the middle, and turn the folded paper sideways. They draw one drawing on the lower half of the paper. They draw the other drawing on the top half, tracing over the lower one, except for the differences.

3   Children now roll the top half tightly round a pencil. Children then move the pencil rapidly from side to side over the top drawing. They see the upper and lower drawings alternately, which seem to move.

4   Children repeat the activity with one of the other drawings, or using their own ideas, so there are as many different drawings as possible. Then they go round the class asking and answering each other:

Example ***What's this girl doing?***
                She's jumping.

5   Repeat step 4 with the other two strips of paper. Encourage children to talk about what they are doing:

Example ***I want to do a ladybird (opening its wings).***

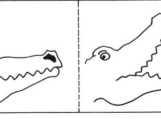
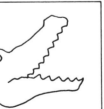

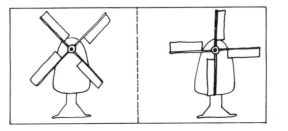

More ideas

A girl waving goodbye	A baby laughing, then crying
A dog wagging its tail	A bird flying/flapping its wings
A boxer punching another boxer	A flag flying in the wind
A bird pulling a worm	A hen pecking at wheat
A woodpecker pecking a tree	A boy pumping water
A lady singing (opening & closing her mouth)	A girl playing on a swing
A seesaw going up and down	A girl skipping
A boy blowing a bubble of gum	Sun shining, then raining

A man hammering a nail/chopping wood/sawing a branch

Adaptation A7a

Children can do this at home. They find an old exercise book, which has nothing written in the top left hand corner of each left hand page or the top right hand corner of each right hand page. They draw the two drawings on alternate pages in the corner on as many pages as they like. As they flick through the pages, the figure seems to move continuously.

A8 Help Alicia Pack

> Deciding what to take on holiday: **needs/doesn't need**
> Clothes and holiday items
> ***because*** and ***too***

S   **7+**

Scissors, coloured pencils, small boxes

C,N

GW

Preparation

Before the lesson, you can ask the children to bring a small box from home, to use as a suitcase. Make copies of pages **C** and **N**, enough for 1 copy of each between 3.

Steps

1   Discuss with the children the kinds of places they have been on holiday. Ask them about the things they took with them (in L1 if necessary).
2   Draw a picture of Alicia on the board or hold up a cutout of her. Draw a palm tree and the sun to add context. Say to the class, *This is Alicia. She's going on holiday to a hot tropical island. She's packing her suitcase and we are going to help her decide what to take.*

3   Put the children into groups of 3. Give 1 copy of pages **C** and **N** to each group. Each group now chooses 6 items from the sheets to cut out and put into Alicia's suitcase.
4   When they have done this, tell them they can think of 2 other things which are not on their copies of **C** and **N**. They should draw these, cut them out, and pack them.
5   When they have all packed their suitcases with 8 items, each group should tell the class what Alicia needs:
    Example   **She needs a sun hat, but she doesn't need an umbrella.**
*   Encourage older children to give reasons for their choice:
    Example   **She doesn't need a warm coat because it is too hot.**

Alternative A8a Alicia's Going to the Mountains

Alternative A8b Alicia's Going to England

Extension A8c Help Alicia Unpack

When clauses with the past simple Clothes and holiday items	S

Tell children Alicia has returned from holiday. Children talk about what she took with her:
Example **When Alicia went to England, she took . . .**

A9 Anna's Going to a Party

Talking about intentions and plans to go out Present continuous and **going to** for future plans and intentions Clothes, colours, places (**party, seaside, football match, shopping, grandmother's house, school** etc.), things to take (**books, a present, an umbrella** etc.)	S

7-10

Coloured pencils

P,N

CW

Preparation

Make copies of page **P** (1 copy is enough for 4 groups) and page **N** (1 copy for each group). Cut the copies of **P** into 4.
Note the difference in use of *going + preposition (to) + place* and *going to + infinitive*.

Steps

1   Hold up a cutout figure from page **P** and give her a name, for example, Anna.
    Say *Anna's going to a party this evening. What is she going to wear?*
2   Children suggest appropriate clothes and preferred colours and things to take:
    (C = child, T = teacher)
    Example   C1 **She's going to wear a blue dress.**
              T *What colour shoes?*
              C2 **Black shoes.**
              T *And what's she going to take with her?*
              C3 **A present.**
              T *What is the present?*
              C4 **(It's) a book.**
3   Repeat with another figure in a different situation if necessary, or go on to working in small groups.
4   Give each group 1 cut-out figure and 1 copy of page **N**. Tell them the name of the figure (or let them invent the name) and the situation, for example, a football match. The group cut out the clothes and other items and colour them appropriately. You can suggest that each child deals with two or three items. Then they dress the figures. Encourage the children to talk about what they are doing:
    Example   C1 **Helen's going to wear shorts.**
              C2 **And a T-shirt.**
              T *What's she going to do?*
              C3 **She's going to play tennis.**
5   (Note that with something planned and definite, we usually use the present continuous form.)
    Call the groups together. Children ask other groups, for example,
    C1 **Who's this? Where's _____ going?**
    C2 **_____'s going to the swimming pool.**
    C3 **What's (s)he going to wear?** etc.
*   Older groups can discuss and write a simple story about their figure. The stories and figures can be displayed on the walls.

Section B Making Things

B1 Making a Fishtank

Pronunciation of /ʃ/ sound, spelt **sh**	W

6–8

Large paper,
glue,
coloured
pencils

D

GW

Preparation

Make copies of page **D**, at least 1 for each child. Keep the ducks for activity B1b, or make 1 copy of **D**, cover the ducks with the fish from this copy, then make copies which have 8 fish on each.

Steps

1 Show a picture of a fish, ask what it is and write the word on the board.
2 Ask the children for more words they know with a /ʃ/ sound in them. Practise with the children pronouncing lots of words with this sound:
   Examples *shoe, short, shine, shone, shore, shut, shout, shop, ship, sheep, sheet, show, she, shell, share, bush, crash, dish, fish, fresh, push, splash, wash, wish.*
3 Explain to the children what they are going to do. Give each group a large sheet of paper. Show them how to make it look like a fish tank by drawing stones, plants and rocks. When their tank is ready, they colour a number of fish from page **D** and cut them out.

4 They stick their fish in the tank. On each fish they write a **sh** word. (You may have to help them and leave words on the board.) If the paper is too dark, they can write round the edge of the tank or stick on labels with the words on.
5 Go round the class to hear children read the words.
* Faster learners can decorate the paper with as many **sh** words as they can think of.
6 Display the tanks if possible.

Note: If photocopying is not available, make copies of the fish from page **D** for the children to draw round. Children can use coloured sticky paper, if available.

Adaptation B1a Balloon Man

Pronunciation of /uː/ sound, spelt **oo** (*ou, ue)	W

Children draw a man holding balloons with **oo** words:

Examples *balloon, boot, cool, food, fool, goose, loose, moon, room* (also pronounced /rʊm/), *roof, noon, spoon, school, shoot, stool, tool,* (you, blue).

Adaptation B1b Duck Pond

Pronunciation of /k/ sound, spelt **ck**	W

D

Children cut out ducks from page **D** and put them on a duck pond:

Examples *back, black, brick, clock, chick, duck, kick, lucky, quack, rocket, sock.*

Note: other variations could include /tr/ words written on train carriages; /əʊ/ words (spelt **ow, o, oe, o-e**) on a snowman; /eə/ words (spelt **air, are, ear**) on different rides in a fairground; /iː/ words (spelt **ee, ea**) on presents hung on a Christmas tree; /ɪə/ words (spelt **eer, ear**) going into the ears of a person's head.

B2 My Own Zoo

Problem solving: where to put animals in the zoo
Modal verbs: **can** for possibility, **can't**
              *****should, mustn't**
Zoo animals; **with, near**

S

8+

A4 paper

Z

PW

Preparation

*Make 1 copy of page **Z** for each pair.

Steps

1   Give each pair a sheet of A4 paper. Tell the children they are going to work in pairs to plan a zoo, which can contain only 12 different types of animal. You may wish to practise names of animals at this stage. You may want to let them choose as a class which 12 animals go in the zoo.

2   Explain that they are allowed 12 different types of animal but they only have 8 cages. They must decide which animals can live together. They also need to think about which animals can live near each other. Show the children how to do this by drawing an example on the board, using the illustration below. Ask questions like: *Can lions live with elephants?*
                    Should camels live near hippos? etc.

3   They should now use their sheet of paper to draw in the cages, leaving room for paths, a toilet, restaurant, etc. You can put an example on the board.

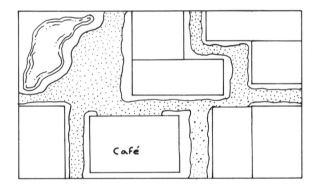

4   Next they should draw in the animals or write in the names or cut out the animals from page **Z** and stick them in.

5   Finally, the pairs should compare their zoos with others.

*   Older children can give reasons for the animals they have chosen and where they have placed them:
    Example   **Lions can live with tigers because they eat the same things.**
              Camels can live with elephants because they are quiet animals.

Note: This activity is a good lead-in for more complex project work on animals, where they come from, what they are like, what they eat.

B3 The Hat Transformer

Following instructions: **fold, cut, turn over, corner, side, inside**

L

9+

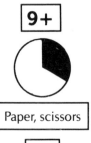

Paper, scissors

IW

Note: Try the activity yourself before doing it in class.

Steps

1   It is helpful if the children understand some of the basic vocabulary of the instructions, but they will understand the general idea without knowing all the vocabulary.

2   Demonstrate with a large sheet of paper as you say the instructions, drawing diagrams on the board if necessary.

Instructions

1   *Make a sheet of paper into a square, by folding one corner to the opposite side and cutting.*

2   *Fold the square in half.*

3   *Fold the top corners towards bottom side, but leave enough paper to fold up in step 4.*

4   *Put your thumbs inside the bottom and fold up a flap.*

5   *Turn over and do the same on the other side, pulling the ends over as well. You now have a hat.*

*   *To transform it into a boat shape, fold the corners behind and attach with paper clips or adhesive tape to keep in position.*

The children can now colour or decorate their hat or boat. To make a larger version, newspaper is ideal.

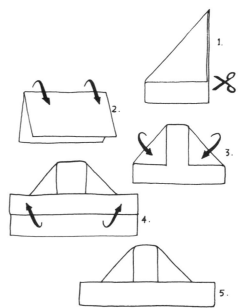

Extension B3a The Bird's Head

By pulling the two ends of the boat/hat together and drawing two eyes on the top, you will have a talking bird.
The bird can be used as a hand puppet, or the children can put them on their heads as a dressing-up activity, if they are made large enough.

B4 The Boat

Following instructions: ***fold, cut, turn over, corner, side, opposite, inside***   L   10+

Note and **Steps:** See activity **B3.**

Instructions

1   *Make your paper into an exact square. Fold one corner to the side, and cut.*

2   *Fold the square in half.*

3   *Fold in half again.*

4   *Fold one corner to the opposite corner.*

5   *Turn over and fold all three corners to the opposite corner.*

Paper, scissors

IW

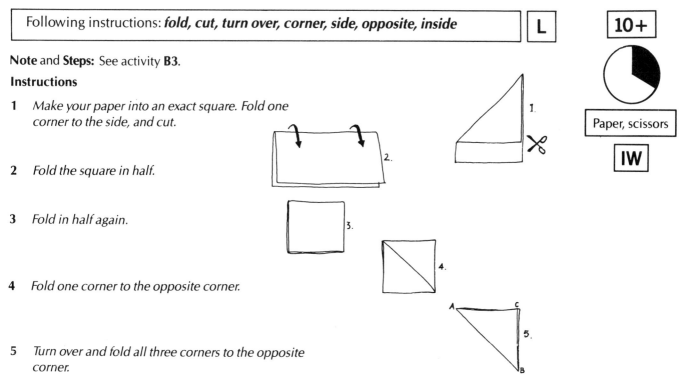

6   *Open the long side with thumbs inside and bring the two points A and B together. Press down to make a square.*

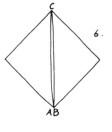
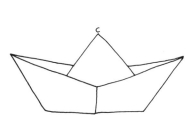

7   *Take the two loose corners at C and pull apart.*

8   *Open the bottom a little so that it stands.*

9   *Colour and decorate the boat.*

B5 Making a Television Set

Asking and talking about pictures and a story	**S**

8+

PW

Preparation

It is a good idea to collect together the materials for this some days before the lesson. Ask the children to bring in toothpaste tops etc.

Steps

1   Show the class how to make TV sets by painting over a cardboard box (a shoe box is best) and sticking toothpaste tops or something similar down the side to look like control knobs.

2   Put the children into pairs, give out the materials and help each pair to make a TV set in the same way.

3   Get the children to cut out pictures from magazines or comics and stick them on the front (the screen). If pictures are not available, children can draw their own and stick these on.

4   In pairs the children invent a story to go with their picture (they do not have to tell it aloud). Two pairs then work together: one pair asks questions about the other pair's picture to discover the story:

Example   ***What's/Who's this?***
                Is he happy?
                What's he doing?

*   More confident children can tell their stories to other pairs and/or the teacher.

*   Older children can write the story and stick it on the top of the TV set, and tell it to other children.

Section C Games with Movement

C1 Numbers Game

Recognition of numbers	L

Steps

1 Write the numbers 1–10 each on separate pieces of A4 paper.
2 Go round the class saying a number to each child, so that there may be 2 children who are number 7, 3 who are number 4 etc.
3 Place the papers with numbers on randomly on the floor. Ask children to find their number and stand by it.
4 Call out numbers at random. Each group must raise their hands. Do this as quickly as possible.

Extension C1a

—Use other numbers, such as 60-70, 90-100.
— Or : call out a number, such as *Five*, or write a number on the board: *5*.
   Children must form themselves into groups containing that number of children. Any remaining children sit down. Continue with different numbers until 2 children remain. They are the winners.
— Or: introduce more complex instructions, e.g. *Make groups of 3 boys and 2 girls.*
   Make groups of 3 with same colour jumper/shirt/eyes.

Adaptation C1b Speaking Version

Consolidation of number recognition

Steps

1 Go round the class saying a number to each child, so that there may be 2 children who are 7, 3 who are 4, etc.
2 Tell children to find others with the same number. Give them the language:
   Example *I'm 3, what number are you?*
   Continue until all the children are in small groups.
4 Call out numbers at random, quickly. When each group hears their number, they repeat it, or put up their hands.

C2 Word Recognition Game

Sight reading of words recently learned	R/L

Steps

1 Write the selected words randomly on the board. Children read them aloud as you write them. Write more words than there are children in the class.
2 Divide the class into 2 teams standing at the back of the class. Give each team a chalk of a different colour.
3 Call out one of the words. The first child in each team runs to the board and circles the word with his coloured chalk.
4 Rub out any wrong circles and call the next word.
5 The team with more circles on the board wins.

Note: If the board is too high, use flashcards stuck onto the wall with sticky tack. The children take a card, but replace any they have wrongly taken. With older children, use the word in a sentence.

Adaptation C2a Word Distinction

Use words with close spellings: **who/how, bread/break, food/foot, spare/spear, from/form, there/three, was/saw, chair/chain.** Call one word at a time.

Adaptation C2b Sound Distinction

Use words with a slight change of sound (minimal pairs): **tree/three, sit/set, path/pass, plate/place, place/plays, hat/heart.** Call one word at a time.

9+

Adaptation C2c Spelling

Use words which sound the same (homophones): **see/sea, red/read, break/brake, witch/which, two/too, be/bee, mail/male, deer/dear, some/sum.**
Here you **must** read the words in a sentence:

9+

Example *I like swimming in the sea.*
I can see the birds.

C3 Shopping Game

Practising vocabulary	L

6+

Preparation

Draw or collect pictures of the vocabulary items you wish to practise.

Steps

1 Tell each child, *You went shopping and you bought _____ .* (One of the items). At least 2 children should have bought the same thing.
2 Place the pictures of vocabulary items randomly on the floor. Ask children to find what they bought and stand by it.
3 Call out *Who bought _____?* Each group must raise their hands. Do this as quickly as possible.
∗ If you want them to practise speaking you can replace steps **2** and **3** by these:
2 Children have to find others who bought the same item:
   Example **I bought a cupboard, what did you buy?**
3 Children can then form larger groups by lexical sets, e.g. those who bought furniture, or clothes, or kitchen utensils, or food.

C4 Time Game

Telling the time Present simple of verbs **get up/have lunch/go to bed**	L

8+

Preparation

Draw clock faces and times on sheets of paper, ranging from, say, 5 o'clock to 10 o'clock.

Steps

1 Tell each child, for example, *You get up at 6 o'clock/You get up at half past 8.* Several children can have the same times.
2 Place the clock faces randomly on the floor. Ask children to find the time they get up and stand by it.

3 Call out, for example, *Who gets up at 9 o'clock?* and, if you wish to practise it,
Who gets up before half past 8/after 7 o'clock?
Who gets up early/late?
The children raise their hands when they recognise their time.
4 You can continue with different activities:
Example *You have dinner at half past 6.*

Note: You can do a similar activity based on what children really do, but often children prefer a
pretend situation to disclosing their family's habits.

Adaptation C4a Speaking Version

Talking about times with activities
Asking ***What time/When do you get up?***   **S**

Steps

1 Tell each child, for example, *You get up at 6 o'clock, You get up at half past 8.*
2 Children have to find others who get up at the same time:
Example ***I get up at 5 o'clock, when do you get up?***
3 Children can then form larger groups of, for example, those who get up before six o'clock,
between six and eight o'clock, after eight o'clock. (Write these on the board.) Finally they form
two groups of those who get up early or late. Let the children discuss and decide which times
are early or late.
* Use other activities: ***go to school/have lunch/have dinner/read a story/go to bed.***

Alternative C4b For Listening and Speaking Versions

Children form groups who: have the same pet at home
have the same number of brothers and sisters
live in the same road/area of the city.

C5 What's My Job?

Guessing occupations by miming
Asking ***Are you a _____?***
      Do you work outside/in an office/with your hands?
Occupations vocabulary   **S**   **7+**

O

TW/GW

Preparation

Make 1 copy of page **O** and cut it into 12 cards for the children to mime.

Steps

1 Mime 1 or 2 of the occupations and ask the children to guess what your occupation is.
Depending on the level of the class they can just use one question, or many different questions
to find out your job.
2 Form two teams **A** and **B** or small groups. Give a card to a member of team **A**. He or she must
mime what is on it without showing the card or saying what is on it. (or children can mime in pairs)
3 Team **B** try to guess what is on the card. If they can, they get 1 point. If not, team **A** try to guess.
If they can, they get 1 point. You can give a time limit of a minute for guessing.
4 Now give a card to a member of team **B**, and continue until no cards are left.

Extension C5a

<table>
<tr><td>Guessing actions
Present continuous **Are you** _____ **ing?**</td><td>S</td><td>6+

M</td></tr>
</table>

Preparation

Make 1 copy of page **M** and cut it into 20 cards.
Check children know the verbs on page **M**.

Steps

Repeat steps 1–4 with cut-outs from page **M**. When they have done a few, children will be able to think of their own. Children can also do it in groups, 1 child at a time thinking of an action.

C6 Robots

<table>
<tr><td>Giving and understanding instructions and directions:
    take a step backward/forward/to the right, turn round</td><td>S</td><td>7+</td></tr>
</table>

Clean scarf

CW

Steps

1. Choose a child to come to the front of the class and blindfold him. Tell the class this child is going to be a robot, the robot is not very clever and cannot see, so they must give him clear instructions.
2. Choose a place to direct the robot to, and give simple instructions:
    Example   *Take two steps forward. Take one step to the left. Turn round.*
3. When you have demonstrated the idea with 2 or 3 robots, let the children take turns at giving instructions. If possible do it in groups.

Note: This would work well in a games/physical education lesson, or in the playground if you have a large class of children.

C7 Simon Says

<table>
<tr><td>Understanding instructions
Verbs of movement: **touch, jump, stand up, sit down, stop**
Parts of the body: **eyes, nose, ears, head, leg, arm, hand**</td><td>L</td><td>6+</td></tr>
</table>

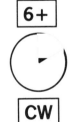

CW

Steps

1. Explain the game **Simon Says** Say *Simon Says touch your nose* and do the action of touching your nose. Explain that they should copy you if you use the words *Simon says* but **not** if you only say *Touch your nose*. Practise several times to revise the language they need, so they know all the actions. You can simplify or expand the language as necessary.
2. Put the children into a circle. Tell them you are going to ask them to do lots of things like *wave your arms, hop on one leg, sit down, put your hands on your head, shake your right hand* or *stop*. Sometimes you will say *Simon says* and sometimes just the action. If they make a mistake, they must leave the circle and help you to watch for others making mistakes. The winner will be the last one left in the circle.
3. The children can take it in turns to play the part of Simon, or do it in pairs until they are more confident.
*   You can also include things in the classroom for variation when they have played the game many times:
    Example   *Touch your chair*
                    Touch a boy's arm
                    Look at the door/board/teacher

C8 Hubble Bubble (a playground game)

Using English stress and rhythm in a chant ***going to*** for future intention the phrase ***in trouble***	**S**	**6–11**

Preparation

Teach the children the chant (below) in the classroom to practise the rhyme and stress.

Steps

1 Divide children into 2 teams. Tell them each team can choose to be **Giants** or **Dwarfs** or **Witches**
   Giants are stonger than Dwarfs – *they can eat them*
   Dwarfs are stronger than Witches – *they can steal their magic*
   Witches are stronger than Giants – *they can turn them into frogs.*

2 Tell each team to go to a 'safe line' on opposite sides of the playground (the playground wall or line of a football pitch) and decide whether they are Giants, Dwarfs or Witches. Explain steps 3 and 4.

3 The teams walk towards the centre until they are 2 metres away, facing each other. Together the children chant
   Hubble Bubble, you're in trouble (they turn around, facing away)
   Hubble Bubble, you're in trouble (they turn around again, facing each other)
   Hubble Bubble, you're in trouble, I'm a _____ (shouting ***GIANT/DWARF/WITCH!***)
   If both teams have chosen to be the same, they shake hands and say:
   Hello friend. You're not in trouble — this time! and return to make another choice. If they are different (they must listen as they call, and react quickly) the stronger chase the weaker:
   Giants chase Dwarfs, calling ***I'm going to eat you.***
   Dwarfs chase Witches, saying ***I'm going to steal your magic.***
   Witches chase Giants, saying ***I'm going to turn you into a frog.***
   Children being chased must run to the safe line.

4 Those who get caught before reaching the safe line, join the opposing team. If the game is repeated until only one child is left on one side, he or she deserves a prize!

Note: If you practise the chant in class, ***eat*** *you* has 1 stressed syllable, ***steal*** *your* ***magic*** has 2, ***turn*** *you* ***into*** *a* ***frog*** has 3.

C9 Are You My Mother?

Matching spoken and written information Present simple: ***Do you live in _____? – Yes, I do*** ***Do you like _____? – No, I don't*** ***I(we) live in _____ ./I(we) like _____ .*** ***Are you tigers/elephants? – Yes, we are*** Animals, animal foods, habitats	**S**	**7+** **CW**

Preparation

Write or make copies of the slips of paper below (**M** for Mother, **B** for Baby), 1 for each child. Half the class will have **M**, half will have **B**. If you have an uneven number of children, make an extra **B** so that one Mother has two Babies. Complete the **M** slips with, for example:

a giraffe	Africa	leaves of tall trees
a lion	Africa	zebras
a zebra	Africa	grass
a tiger	India	deer
a squirrel	trees	nuts

a whale	the sea	plankton
a seal	the sea	fish
a panda	China	bamboo leaves
a polar bear	near the North Pole	fish
a penguin	near the South Pole	fish
an owl	trees	mice
a cow	farm	grass
a brown bear	America	anything

Complete the first two parts only of the B slips.

M   You are _____   **B**   You live in _____

You live in _____   You like eating _____

You like eating _____   What are you? _____

1 Make sure children know all the animals you are practising, and the names of what they eat. Do not discuss where they live and what they eat too thoroughly, as this can make step 5 rather pointless.

2 Divide the class in 2. Tell the children that one half are baby animals, the other half are mother (or father) animals. Each baby has to find its mother by asking 2 questions. You can write the questions on the board:
Do you live in _____?   *Do you like eating _____?*
If both answers are YES they should say,
You're my mother!/You're my baby!

3 Give the slips of paper to the children, **M** to one half, **B** to the other half. Tell the babies to go round the class to find their mother by asking the questions on the board with the information on their slip. (You can ask them to guess what animal they think they are before they start, and to see if their guess is right.)
It is better if all children stand and move around.

4 Children who have found their pair sit down or stand at one side until all babies have found their mothers.

5 When the class are sitting down, each mother and baby pair asks other children to guess what they are by saying where they live and what they eat:
Example   C1 and C2 We live in _____. We like eating _____.
             C3 Are you tigers?
          C1 and C2 No we aren't./Yes we are.

Section D Stories and Speaking Activities

D1 Introducing Myself

| Making simple introductions and learning names | S |

Steps

1   Introduce yourself by saying *Hello, my name is* _____.
    Each child in turn does the same.
2   Put the children in a large circle. Say *Hello, my name is* _____.
    The child on the left of you says **Hello, my name is** _____ **and this is** _____
    (introducing you). The next child says **Hello, my name is** _____, **this is** _____
    and this is _____. This continues with each child introducing himself and all the
    others who have gone before.

Note: If the class is very large the children could make 2 or 3 circles.

CW

D2 Answer a Riddle

| What, Which, Who questions | S |

8 +

Riddles can be used at the end of a lesson, or can be set as a task for children to try to solve at home
by asking family and friends. You can encourage children to invent their own. Riddles like numbers
3 and 4 below are easier and great fun.
—   Ask the riddle, and give children time to discuss it before giving the answer.
—   Explain any use of words they do not understand.
—   Practise asking the riddle in pairs. They can try it on other friends learning English.

PW

1   Which is the shortest month? — *May, it only has 3 letters*

2   Which stars wear dark glasses? — *film stars*

3   What is red and goes up and down? — *a strawberry in a lift*

4   What has six legs, two arms and two heads? — *a man on a horse*

5   What goes up but never comes down? — *your age*

6   What comes down but never goes up? — *rain*

7   What is the difference between here and there? — *the letter* **t**

8   What gets bigger when you turn it upside down? — *number 6*

9   What gets bigger when you take more away? — *a hole*

10 Which is the strongest day of the week? — *Sunday, all the rest are weekdays (weak days)*

11 What runs but never walks? — *water*

12 Who always sleeps with his shoes on? — *a horse*

13 What has teeth but can't eat? — *a comb*

14 What has a face, two hands and goes round? — *a clock*

15 What did the little watch hand say to the big watch hand? — *I'll be back in an hour*

16 What does everyone in the world do at the same time? — *grow older*

17 What is black and white and read (pronounced 'red') all over? — *a newspaper*

18 What gets wetter the more it dries? — *a towel*

19 The more there is, the less you see — what is it? — *darkness*

20 What goes 99-thump-99-thump? — *a centipede with a wooden leg*

D3 Filling up the Shop

> Practising vocabulary:
>   shops and items in them (food, clothes etc.)
> **can buy**
> *Developing spelling

S

6–9

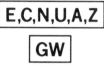

Large paper,
scissors,
coloured
pencils,
sticky tack,
*magazines

E, C, N, U, A, Z

GW

Preparation

Make copies of pages **E, C, N, A, Z** and **U,** 1 for each group, or bring in magazines for the children to cut up.

Steps

1   Ask the children for the names of different types of shops, by asking
    Where can you buy shoes? Where can you buy meat?
2   Print the names of 5 or 6 types of shop on a large sheet of paper (preferably stiff paper or card), for example, BUTCHER'S, BAKER'S, PET SHOP, SHOE SHOP, GREENGROCER'S, NEWSAGENT'S. Fix these to the walls around the room.
3   Talk about the things you can buy in each shop, eliciting as much as possible from the children. Encourage them to use sentences like:
    You can buy chicken at a butcher's.
4   Put the children in groups, 1 group for each shop. Give out the materials and explain that they are going to fill the shops with goods. Show them how to draw and cut out pictures of items that can go in the shop or give copies of the pages you have photocopied or pages from magazines for children to colour and cut out.
5   Let the children stick their pictures onto the large sheet of paper representing the shop. If they use sticky tack, the pictures can be removed for other activities.
*   They can also write the words on pieces of paper and stick them by the pictures.

Extension D3a Going Shopping

Preparation

(After stage 4 of **D3**)
— Practise the sentences children will need:
Examples   **I'd like some _____ .**
             Have you got any _____ ?
             How much is/are _____ ?
             I'm sorry, we haven't any _____ .
— The teacher can either put prices on the pictures or write price lists before the activity, or ask the children to do this. During the activity they can use real money, toy money, or the paper money on page **B**.
— The children can work in small groups of about 4 and take turns at being shopkeepers and customers.

Extension D3b Planning a Party

Steps

1   Tell the children they are going to plan a surprise party for their best friend. In pairs get them to write a list of people they would like to invite, and a shopping list for the party including items like food, drink, balloons, presents.
2   Choose 3 different shops from **D3** and ask 3 or 4 children to be shopkeepers in each shop. The other children now visit the shops in pairs and buy the things they need.
3   At the end of the lesson ask some of the children to tell the class what they have bought, and what they didn't manage to find.

Note: You can ask older children to make a note of how much their shopping cost in **D3a** and **b**, if they are confident with numbers and adding up.

D4 Fun with Animals

> Animal names
> * past tenses: **was, were, arrived, came** etc.
>   **was/were** _____ **ing**

S 6+

Z/A

CW

Preparation

Make a copy of page **Z** and cut out the individual animals.

Steps

Tell a little story about the animals. You can vary the story each time you tell it. When you get to the name of an animal, don't say the name but hold up the picture. The class should all say the name:

One day an (**elephant**) was walking through the jungle when he saw a (**deer**). The (**deer**) was running away from a fierce (**lion**). The (**elephant**) felt sorry for the (**deer**) and helped him to hide. They became close friends and spent a lot of time together.

One day a letter arrived at the (**elephant's**) house. It was from the (**hippo**) inviting the (**elephant**) and the (**deer**) to come to a birthday party for the (**bear**). They were both very excited at the thought of meeting all the other animals.

The day of the party arrived and all the animals were there. The (**peacock**) and the (**flamingo**) were the first to arrive, looking very fine indeed. Soon after came the (**rhino**), carrying a very big birthday present for the (**bear**). Then came the big stripy (**tiger**) with a great big birthday cake. He was followed by the (**camel**) who was carrying the (**crocodile**) on his back. Next came the (**kangaroo**) hopping along, carrying a small (**penguin**) in his pouch. From the other direction came the (**seal**) balancing a large red ball on his nose and the gentle (**giraffe**) with the very long neck. The (**monkey**) swung down from a tree and the (**snake**) came sliding through the grass. In fact all the animals were invited to the party except for one, and do you know who that was? Of course, it was the (**lion**). Nobody liked him because he was always chasing the other animals.

A little way off the (**lion**) was sitting by himself feeling very unhappy. He could hear the songs and laughter from the party. So he went to the edge of the jungle and said, 'Please let me come to the party.' No one spoke except the kind old (**elephant**), who thought that perhaps the (**lion**) wasn't really so bad. 'Well,' he said, 'if you promise never to chase any other animals, you can come.' The (**lion**) was so pleased at making all these new friends that to this day he has never chased anyone again through that jungle.

* Children can retell the story, or retell it making their own variations (it will obviously be much shorter). Do not insist on grammatical accuracy, as long as they get the animals right and it is possible to understand the story generally.

Adaptation D4a

Preparation

Make copies of page **Z**, 1 for each child.

Steps

1   Give out the sheets and ask the children to cut out the individual animals. They should lay these out face up in front of themselves.
2   Tell an animal story as in **D4**. This time say the animal's name. As children hear the name of the animal, they hold up the picture of the animal.
    Alternatively teach the class the sounds the various animals make.
    Examples   **cat — miaow, dog — woof woof, lion — roaaar, cow — moo, pig — oink oink, sheep — baa, mouse — squeak.**
    Tell a little story about the animals, but make the noises instead of saying the animal's name. As the children hear the animal noises they call out the name of the animal.
    Example   One day a big woof woof was chasing a tiny miaow. . .
Note: You will find other variations to suit your class. For example, you can pre-teach mime gestures for the animals (use less than the example), and some other words like hide, running, hopping, tree, unhappy. and make sure they are all repeated two or three times in your version of the story.

D5 Uncle Henry's House

Describing what's wrong:
> **The bed is in the kitchen**
> **There's an elephant in the bedroom**

What's wrong?
Rooms, furniture, *animals, prepositions
Understanding of **odd** (= strange), **funny** (= strange or amusing).

S

H,F,A /Z

GW

Preparation

From a copy of pages **H** and **F** (and **A**, **Z**, for amusement), make up a nonsense house, with a bed in the kitchen, fridge in the bathroom, an elephant in the bedroom etc. Make copies of this nonsense house, enough for 1 between 4.

Steps

1   Give out the copies to each group of 4 children. Let them talk about it, in English if possible, for 1 or 2 minutes.
2   Tell them it is your Uncle Henry's house. (He is English.) He is not mad/crazy but his house is very different to normal houses. It's a funny house. Ask them how many things they can find wrong in the house. Then ask them to say what is wrong.
3   Expect children to reply **The _____ is in the _____.** Add appropriate comments such as *That's odd*, or *Isn't that funny?*
*   Elicit where the item should or shouldn't be, by asking:
    Example   *What's wrong with having the bed in the kitchen?* or
    　　　　　Why can't the bed be in the kitchen?
    They reply **You can't sleep in the kitchen**, or
    　　　　　You (should) sleep in the bedroom (not in the kitchen).
4   Lead to the class or group talking about where things are in their own houses:
    (T = teacher, C = child)
    Example   T   *What's in your bedroom?*
    　　　　　　C1   **There's a bed and a chair.**
    　　　　　　C2   **And a cupboard.**
    　　　　　　C3   **I've got a table.**

D6 Story-telling with Puppets

Inventing and telling stories
Past (or present) tense

S

6–10

Coloured pencils, stick/straw

P

PW/GW

Preparation

Make copies of page **P**, 1 for each pair or group.

Steps

1   Give a set of figures to each pair or group. Tell the children to draw in the clothes and to colour them.
2   Give each pair or group either a drinking straw or lollipop stick for each figure. Ask them to glue the straw or stick to the back of each figure. They now have stick puppets which they can move about.
3   Get the pairs or groups to make up a short story and to tell it, using the puppets. You can specify which tense they should use. Supply suitable ideas if necessary:
    Example   A story including a zoo and a bear/an ice cream and a monkey/a big tree and visiting your grandmother.
4   The children can also draw background scenery, if they wish to, on sheets of plain A4 paper. A shop or a railway station, for example, will help to make the stories more realistic.

30

5 The children can also draw different figures of different sizes and use the same technique for puppet making.

6 At the end of the lesson, invite each group to tell their story to another group or, if they are happy to do so, to the rest of the class.

As the aim is to give them confidence and enjoyment, do not insist on absolute accuracy or correct mistakes during their stories. Make a note and correct only serious errors afterwards.

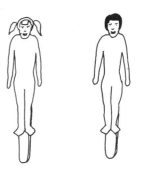

Note: A different way of making the puppets is by telling the children to wrap a figure around one of their fingers which can be kept in place by an elastic band or piece of cotton. The children can then use their finger puppets in the same way as the stick puppets.

D7 Dealing a Story

> Making a story
> Verbs of action (past/present tenses)

S **9+**

M

PW

Preparation

Make copies of page **M**, 1 for 8 children, and cut each into 20 cards.

Steps

1 Give 5 cards randomly to each pair, making sure all 5 are different. Tell them to make up a simple story, which must include the 5 actions they have. You can specify whether they should use past tense or present.

2 Give them 10 minutes to think of a story (they do not have to write anything), then they can tell their stories to other pairs, or the class.

* More advanced children can write the story and illustrate it with the pictures, which you can then display.

D8 Scrambled Cards

> Describing pictures: **there is/are**
> **I can see** _____
> **She is** _____ **ing**
> **I want your picture, please./I don't want it, thank you.**
> Telling short stories * and sequencing events (**then, next**).

S **8+**

S

GW

Preparation

Make copies of page **S**, enough for 1 between 3, and cut them into picture cards.

Steps

1 Shuffle the cards and give one set to each group. Each child in each group should now take 4 cards.

2 Explain that the aim is to get 4 cards which form part of the same story. They will do this by describing 1 card in turn, which one of the group can choose to take if it seems to form part of a story with one or more other pictures the child is holding.

3 —C1 describes one of the four cards, hiding the picture from the others.

—After describing it as fully as possible, C1 asks C2 if he wants the card.

—If C2 wants the card, he takes it. If C2 does not want the card, C1 offers it to C3.

—If neither of the other two want the card, C1 must keep it, and describe another card.

—If C3 wants it, he takes it.

—The child who takes the card now describes one of his other cards, and the child on the left has the first choice to accept it.

Note: Children should understand that the card they describe is one they want to give away, not to keep.

4 — The game continues until one of the children has 4 cards which form a story.
   — This child places the cards face up on the table in the correct order and tries to tell the story to the other two. If a child has problems, then the others can make suggestions to help.

* Follow up the game by some class oral composition, perhaps followed by written work with older children.

D9 Island Fun

Making suggestions: **Let's take** _____ Agreeing and Disagreeing: **That's (not) a good idea.** **(No, a _____ is better).** * Describing uses of objects.	**S** **9+**

A4 paper

GW

Steps

1. Tell the class about Robinson Crusoe, who was marooned on a desert island, or read the story to set the scene.
2. Tell the children to imagine they are on a large ship which is slowly sinking in the middle of the ocean. Drawings on the board will help to bring this alive.
3. Tell them they can see an island in the distance. The ship is floating towards the island but will probably sink before it reaches the shore. They may be stuck on the island for several months before another ship passes. They can take 4 things with them from the ship. They should be things they can carry.
4. Give each child a sheet of paper and ask them to write down or draw the 4 items to take to the island, for example, a favourite toy, a radio, a penknife. They can choose anything within reason, but it should not be food, as there is plenty on the island. Give them the English words when they ask, encouraging them to say **What's _____ in English?**
5. When they have finished this, put the children in groups of 3 and tell them things have changed and each group can now only take 4 things between them. Give each group 10–15 minutes to decide which items to take and which to leave:
   Example   **Let's take a football. (We can play with it.)**
6. When they have done this, each group tells the class what they are taking:
   Example   **We're taking a torch, a football, a television and an ice cream machine.**
                     We're not taking Mario's penknife, Francesca's radio . . .
* Ask *Why are you taking a torch?* They can give reasons:
   Example   **(We're taking a torch) to see/so we can see at night.**
                     (We're taking a football) to play with.
* Discuss with the class how some items can have many uses:
   Example   *You can use a mirror to signal and make a fire.*

Extension D9a Survival

Future plans: **will/going to** Time sequencers: **first, then, next, in the morning/afternoon** Verbs (activities)	**S**

1. In pairs or groups tell the children to decide on the first 6 things they will do when they reach the island. (They can use both **will** and **going to** for variation.)
2. Tell them to plan their first day on the island:
   Example   **First, we'll have breakfast.**
                     Then, we're going to build a small house.
                     In the afternoon we'll go fishing.

Extension D9b Rescue

| Telling/writing a story
Past tenses | **S/W** |

Get the children to imagine they have just been rescued after spending a month on the island. Ask them to tell or write a story describing the island and their experiences. They can make drawings to illustrate their stories.

Adaptation D9c Journey into Space

— Tell the children they are going to travel through space to discover new worlds. Ask them again to decide on what to take with them. Let them choose 5 items individually, apart from food and water, then groups of 3 should decide on a combined list of 5 items.
— If they have problems thinking of things you could make suggestions:
  Example Items of clothing (a warm coat, boots, a tee-shirt . . .), sleeping bag or blankets, sunglasses, toothbrush, soap, towel, first aid kit, tent, umbrella, football, card game, book, paper and pencils.

  You can add any extra information you like to help them.

D10 Silly Street

| Describing a situation
Present continuous
Bicycle, motorbike, car, van, bus, lorry, helicopter
Crossing, crossroads, pavement, traffic lights, road
Verbs: ***drive, ride, park, play, land, steal/take***
Adjectives: ***wrong, dangerous, silly*** | **S** |

Preparation

Make copies of page **V**, 1 between 2.

Steps

1 Give 1 copy of page **V** to each pair. Revise the vocabulary, or teach it if not known. One way to do this is to write the words on the board, and tell children to take it in turns saying to their partners, ***Show me the _____.***
  If children do not know a word, give a simple definition:
  Example *People walk on the **pavement**.*
          ***Traffic lights** are red, orange and green.*
          *People walk across the road on a **crossing**.*
2 Tell children to point to someone in the picture and ask their partners in turn:
  Example ***What's this man/woman/boy/girl doing?***
  Help children to use the correct verbs, such as **land** instead of **going/coming.**
3 Point to and describe an action:
  Example *He's riding a motorbike on the pavement.*
  Ask children to comment on it:
  Example ***That's wrong/dangerous.***
* Children take it in turns to describe an action and comment on it:
  Example C1 ***He's not looking in front.***
          C2 ***That's dangerous.***

Extension D10a Road Safety

> Commenting on a situation:
> **should, shouldn't**
> (and see **D10**)

S

9+

V

PW

Preparation

Make copies of page **V**, 1 between 2.

Steps

1   Give 1 copy of page **V** to each pair. Revise the language of **D10**, telling the children there are
    12 things which people are doing wrong or are dangerous. In pairs, each child says to the other
    6 sentences about 6 things that people are doing wrong:
    Example   *A woman is riding a motorbike on the pavement*
    (You can ask them to put a circle round each one as they say a sentence to each other, if you
    don't want to use the copies again.)
2   Check the 12 actions with the whole class.
3   Elicit what they should and shouldn't do.
    Example   *A woman's riding a motorbike on the pavement. She shouldn't ride it on the
              pavement. She should ride it on the road.*
    They can use the present perfect tense, if they know it:
    Example   ***A boy has kicked a ball into the road. He shouldn't play on the pavement. He
              should play in the park.***
4   Ask each pair to write a Safety Code on how to behave properly in the street, using **You should/
    shouldn't** _____ . (With older children, some pairs can write a code for drivers, some
    for cyclists, some for pedestrians.)
5   Get the pairs to give their ideas to the class. Write the best ones on the board for children to
    copy and illustrate. Children can make a Safety Poster to display in the school.

D11 Locations

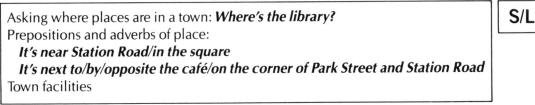

Introduction – brainstorm all location words.

> Asking where places are in a town: ***Where's the library?***
> Prepositions and adverbs of place:
> ***It's near Station Road/in the square***
> ***It's next to/by/opposite the café/on the corner of Park Street and Station Road***
> Town facilities

S/L

10+

R,Y

PW/GW

Preparation

Make 1 copy of page **R** and 1 copy of **Y** for each pair or group of 4.

Note: Give the children lots of practice before starting the activity, so that they are confident using
the phrases.

Steps

1   Make sure that each child or pair is working with someone with a different sheet.
    Ask them all *Where is the café?*
    Expect the reply ***In Green Avenue*** from children with page **Y**.
2   Elicit more information with *Where exactly?* Expect the reply ***Opposite the park***. Those with
    page **R** can write **café** on their map.
3   Repeat with the cinema ***(in the square, on the corner* of West Street and Station Road)***. Those
    with **Y** can write **cinema** on their map.

4 — On the board, write the names of all the buildings which are **not on both maps.** Explain that they should ask about the buildings which are **not** marked on their map, to find out where they are. You could write 1 list for page **R** and 1 list for page **Y**. Tell the children which places they both know so that they can use these for reference. Unless you alter the map, these will be: the station, the clock tower, the restaurant and the park.

— As they find out where each building is, they write the name in the correct place on the map.

— The next child has a turn. They continue taking it in turns. (If the whole process takes too long, you can put a time limit on the activity. You can also fill in some of the names before you photocopy so the children have fewer questions to ask and answer.

Note: at the corner is also acceptable, if children use it.

D12 Directions

> Understanding and giving directions:
> *Go along* _____ *road.*
> *Turn left/right at the crossroads/corner/post office.*
> *It's on the left/right, opposite/next to the* _____ *.*
> *It's (the second building) on the left.*
> Town facilities: *swimming pool, café, hospital, police station, town hall, library, pet shop, bus station, supermarket, playground*

S/L   10+   R   GW

Preparation

Make 1 copy of page **R** and fill in the names of **all** the buildings on the map (refer to page **Y**).
Make enough copies of this map for 1 between 2 children.
∗ Counters or model cars/figures to move around map.

Steps

1 Put the children in groups of 4. Give each group 1 copy of the map. Tell them they have to follow your directions on the map with a finger (or their counter). They should not write on the map.

2 Example *Start from the station . . . Go along to the end of Station Road . . . Turn right at the crossroads into Park Street . . . It's the second building on the left . . . Where are you?*
Speak slowly and give plenty of time for the children to discuss the route with each other:
Example **No, not that way, turn right.**
  Can you repeat it, please?
At the end ask the groups *Where are you?* If more than one group has made a mistake, repeat it again, making sure they all follow the route.

3 Give 1 child in each group another copy of the map and explain that they should secretly mark on — in pencil — a route from one place to another (or you can tell them the route to mark on):
Example *From the hospital to the cinema.*
The child should put the map inside a book or file so that the others cannot see it.

4 The child now gives directions, as in step 2, repeating as necessary. The other 3 children follow the route on their map.

5 Another child rubs out the first route and draws on a different one.

Note: From step 3 onwards the group can work in two pairs if you prefer, with 2 children describing the route and 2 following it on the map.

Adaptation D12a Asking Directions

Asking for and understanding directions
Can you tell me the way to_____?
Town facilities

S

R,Y

PW/GW

Preparation

Make 1 copy of page **R** and 1 copy of **Y** for each pair or group of 4. (If you prefer to make the activity easier and shorter, fill in some of the names of places on pages **R** and **Y** so the children have fewer questions to ask and answer.)

Steps

1 — Give a copy to each pair or group of 4 children. Tell the children *I don't know this town. You live here. I'm at the station. I want to go to the cinema. I meet you and say, 'Excuse me, can you tell me the way to the cinema?'*
   — Get the children to repeat the question several times, breaking the sentence into three or four parts — start with the last 3 words and add 2 more each time until they can say the complete sentence.
2 Repeat with other places. Give lots of practice.
3 Elicit possible replies and correct any incorrect instructions. Practise the questions and answers across the class and in pairs as a dialogue with the examples you have already used:
   (C = child or pair)
   Example   C1 **Excuse me, can you tell me the way to the post office?**
             C2 **Yes. Go along Station Road . . . Turn right into Park Street . . . Then turn left . . . It's in the square, on the right.**
             C3 **Is it next to the clock?**
             C2 **No, it isn't.**
             C1 **Is it next to the police station?**
             C2 **I don't know/Yes, it is.**

4 Write 2 lists of places on the board, one for **R** and one for **Y**. These should include only the buildings which are **not** marked on their map. Tell them which places they both know, so that these can be used as reference points (these are the station, the clocktower, the restaurant , the police station, the hospital and the park, plus any you have added).
5 When the children do the activity in pairs (or groups of 4), C1 then writes **post office** on the building he thinks is the post office. Then C2 asks for directions. The children (individually or in pairs) take it in turns to ask and answer. At the end of the activity, children compare their town plans to see if they have the correct places.

Section E Writing Activities

E1 Alphabet Tree

Practising the alphabet and building vocabulary	W

6–9

IW/PW

Steps

1   Tell the children to draw a tree with 8–12 branches in their book (each one will have 2–4 nests on, so make the branches long enough). Show them how to do this with an example on the board (see below).

2   They should now start at the top and draw lots of birds' nests, 26 in total — one for each letter of the alphabet.

3   They must write something beginning with **a** in one nest, something beginning with **b** in another and so on until all the nests are full. You may have to help with q, x, z, for example, or leave the nests empty.

Note: Younger learners can work in pairs or small groups. Instead of writing the name of the item they can draw a small picture.

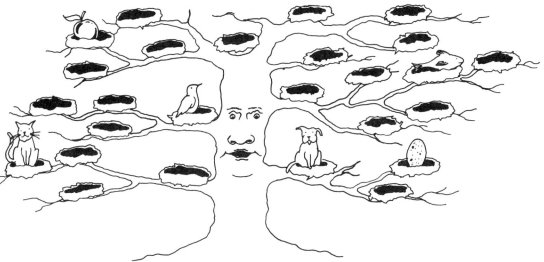

Adaptation E1a Alphabet Picnic

—   Ask the children to draw a large picnic basket. In the basket they either draw or write the names of different things to take on a picnic, one from each letter of the alphabet.

—   Again, they will probably not be able to use all of the letters. Allow some freedom — not all items need be food or drink.

Adaptation E1b The Big Apple

—   Ask the children to decide on a letter that they would like to work with.

—   They now draw something beginning with that letter. This should take up most of a page. Inside the object they now write or draw as many things as they can beginning with that letter.

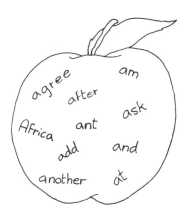

Adaptation E1c Crazy Cats and Silly Snakes

Practising adjectives	**W**

9

Coloured pencils

Steps

1   Draw the letter **C** on the board. Show the class how to make it look like a cat using the example below. Do the same again with **S** to make a snake.
2   Ask the children for adjectives to go with the pictures. The adjective must begin with the same letter:
    Examples **c**o**s**y/**c**urious/**c**ute **c**at; **s**low/**s**illy/**s**lippery **s**nake.
3   Get the children to copy the examples from the board.
4   Now ask the children to choose another letter and to make it into a drawing in the same way.
5   When they have done this, they can colour it in.
6   They now write the name underneath and add an adjective as well. For example, a child may turn **T** into a telephone and call it 'tired telephone'.

SILLY SNAKE

COSY CAT

(Over a course of lessons it would be possible to cover all or most of the letters of the alphabet.)

E2 Labelling

Matching words and meaning; spelling	**W**

A/Z

Preparation

Make copies of page **A** or **Z**, enough for 1 for each child.

Steps

1   Write the names of the animals on the board in random order.
2   Tell the children to match the word and the picture by writing the name of the animal under the picture to which it belongs.
*   They can cut out and stick the labelled animal pictures in their books.

Alternative E2a

Preparation

Make 1 copy of page **T**. Draw boxes next to each picture, big enough to write the word in.
Make copies of this master sheet, 1 for each child.
Ask children to write the words in the boxes. If they need help, you can write the words on the board, either correctly, or with the letters jumbled:
Example   for *teddy* write *ddyte*.

T

Alternative E2b

Preparation

Make 1 copy of page **V**. Draw arrows to the items you want the class to practise. Make copies of this master sheet, 1 for each child.
Ask children to label the items you have drawn in. Again, you may decide to write the words on the board.

Note: You can do these activities with many of the photocopiable pages.

V

E3 Word Squares

General vocabulary and spelling patterns	W

Preparation

Take a blank box square from page **X.** Write words vertically, horizontally, according to age and ability, or diagonally, in the box square. These words should be linked in some way:

    1 Lexical sets, such as animals, food, furniture

    2 Words recently met in a story

    3 Grammatical sets, such as verbs, adjectives

When you have as many words as you want, fill in the remaining blank squares with letters at random. Photocopy this master page, making enough for 1 square for each child or pair.

Steps

— Children can work individually or in pairs.

— They circle the words they can find. (Either set a target, for example, to find 10 words, or set a time limit and get children to compare their list with others.)

Adaptation E3a Making Up Words

Preparation

Make copies of page **X,** so that each child has a 10 x 10 box square.

Steps

1   — Give each child a box square. The children take it in turns to call out letters.

    — As the letters are called, the children write each letter in turn in any one of the squares until the whole box is full.

    — Children can place the letters randomly but it is better if they plan the words they would like to spell. They will be able to make some of the words successfully, but not others.

2   Tell the children they must now find as many words as possible in their box. There will be some words which they tried to make, but also others they have made by chance. They can read across or down. Older children can manage diagonal words.

t	e	l			p		t		
o	o				i				
c	a	p			n				
					k				
b		g							
r	e								
					q				
m	e	a							
		d			s	o	u		

E4 Crosswords

Vocabulary and spelling | W

A4 paper

IW/PW

Crosswords are difficult to compile, but these simple 3 x 3 and 4 x 4 crosswords are easy to make up. Later, children can make them up to try on their friends.

Steps

1   Draw 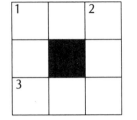 on the board.
Ask children to draw it
neatly on paper.

2   While they are doing this, write the clues on the board.
Clues can be of 4 types:

Example

Across 1:

(Picture)

3: (the word **own** in your language)   (Translation)

Down 1: *I've got 3 pens, but you've only got* _____ . (Context gap-filling)

2: *Something to write with.*   (Definition)

Answer: T A P
          W   E
          O W N

Other possibilities:

```
E A T   S U N   B A G   F A N   Y E S   B A D   R A T   B O W   I L L
N O     A O     U A     A E     O E     I I     E O     U A     N O
D A Y   D O T   Y E S   R O W   U S E   G O D   D I P   S I X   K I T

P R A Y   F E L L   P R A M   S P I N   B A N D   R E S T
A   E     E   I     U   E     L   E     A   O     E     E
R   R     L   L     S   N     I   E     N   N     A     S
T E L L   T O L D   H O L D   P A I D   K N E E   L A S T
```

E5 Acrostics

Lexical and grammatical sets

Preparation

— Choose the word set you wish to practise, for example, jobs, and make an acrostic as follows (you can use half a box square from page **X** and black out the squares you don't need):
  Write a member of the set downwards (see number 6). Incorporate each letter in a member of the set.
— Make clues for each word (see below and **E4**) but not for the vertical word. You can often practise a further language point, such as *is used for*.

Steps

Draw the grid squares for your acrostic on the board without the words. (Children copy from the board or you can give them copies of page **X**.) Write the clues and tell children to find the vertical (down) word.

Clues

1 He makes machines or bridges.
2 He looks after buildings or money.
3 She sees us when we are ill.
4 He delivers letters.
5 She works in a school.
  What does 6 do?

Ideas Any vocabulary set: food, furniture, containers . . .
Everyday activities: washing, reading, playing . . .
Verbs of motion; prepositions; adjectives.

E6 Word by Word

Spelling and vocabulary

Preparation

Make copies of page **X,** so that each pair has a 10 x 10 box square.

Steps

1 Give a box square to each pair. C1 now writes a word in the box, putting one letter in each square. C2 must now write a new word, using the first or last letter from C1's word. He can write this vertically or horizontally.
2 C1 must now write a word, using the first or last letter from any of the previous words (except any letter previously used).
3 They continue until neither child can think of another word.

E7 Shapes from Words

Connecting words and meanings	W

A4 paper

PW

Steps

1   Draw these examples on the board and explain that you are making a design with the word so that it looks like what it means:

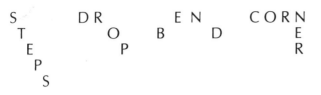

```
S            D R        E N        C O R N
 T              O      B      D          E
  E              P                        R
   P
    S
```

2   Ask children to think of more words they could use in this way (rain, away, look, bump, balloons, measles, stretch, horse, lift, sandwich). In pairs they can work on their own examples. They can colour and decorate their designs, and then display them.

*   Older children can make up posters and advertisements using their ideas.

E8 Football Poem

Practising collocations and associated words	W

A4 paper

IW/PW

Steps

1   Draw a large football on the board. Ask children about football, and write up the words, phrases and sentences they say.

2   Select some of these and write them inside the football, if possible fitting the words to the shape.

3   Tell the children they can make any drawing they like and write a little poem inside. You can give them suggestions:
an ice cream cone; a snake or other animal; a tree; a flower; a violin; a book; an item of food; a train; a boat; a bicycle wheel; a bell.
It is not necessary for the children to make rhymes.

4   Children show their drawings and read their poems to the class. Display the work if possible.

*tap tap
kick the ball
run, run, fun, fun,
score a goal. How
I love football so.
Blow the whistle
he's off side
Goal!*

Section F Discovery Activities

F1 Putting My Toys Away

> Describing where things are in a room
> Prepositions *in, on, under, next to, behind, in front of*
> Toys and bedroom furniture

Scissors, glue, coloured pencils

Note: The kind of language used will depend on the age and level of the children. For a simpler version of this activity, see Adaptation **F1a**.

Preparation

Make copies of page **T**, 2 for each child.

Steps

1 — Give one copy to each child. Tell the children they must decide where they are going to put their toys.
   — They can either draw in the toys, or they can cut out the toys from the bottom of their copy, colour them, and stick them in. (If you want to shorten the lesson time, or make it easier for younger children, ask them to choose 4–5 toys only.)
2 Each child now does this on his sheet; for example, puts the teddy on the bed, the blackboard next to the toy box, and so on. The children should hide their pages behind an open book or file so that their partner cannot see it.
3 When they have done this, give each child another copy of page **T**. Now put the children into pairs. Child 1 now tells Child 2 where he has placed his toys, by saying, for example, *My ball is in the toy box, my boat is under my bed, the train is behind the bed*.
   C2 listens to C1 and draws the toys on his second picture in the places that C1 has said. When C1 has finished, C2 does the same and C1 draws the toys on his second picture as he listens to C2.
4 Finally, the children compare their pictures to see if they match.

Adaptation F1a

Preparation

Make 2 copies of page **T**. Put 5 toys on 1 copy and 5 on the other, in different places. Make enough copies for half the children to have one copy and half to have the other copy.

Steps

— Either write the 2 lists of toys on the board — the children have to ask about the toys they **haven't** got on their page (**Where's the teddy?** etc) and their partner describes the position for the other to draw on, or
— children simply describe the position of 2 or 3 toys in turn, while their partner draws or writes the names of the toys in the correct position.

F2 Finding Differences

> Describing things
> Asking and answering questions
> Prepositions and adverbs of place

H,T

PW

Preparation

— Make 2 copies of page **H** or page **T**. One will be page **a** and one page **b**
— On page **a** draw in 6 to 10 items, depending on class level, such as a tiger on a bed, a teddy on a chair or cut out from pages **F, Z, A**. On page **b** draw half of the items in exactly the same place, but the other half in different positions.
— Make enough copies so that half the class have page **a** and half page **b**.

Steps

1   Put the children into pairs and give page **a** to child 1 and page **b** to child 2. Make sure they can't see each other's page. (They can put them inside books or files.) Tell the children that the pictures are nearly the same, but there are some differences. (Tell them how many.)

2   Explain that they must now find the differences by telling each other what is in their picture, and by asking and answering questions:

Example   C1   ***In my picture there's a teddy on a chair.***
             C2   ***Is there a cup on the table?***
             C1   ***No, there isn't.***

3   When the pairs think they have found all the differences, they compare their pictures to see if they are correct:

Example   ***There's a teddy here, but a lion there.***

4   At the end of the lesson ask the class to tell you the differences they have found.

Note: You can use the same basic picture a number of times by changing the items you add and their positions. You can include groups of items to practise lexical sets, for example, containers, toys.

Adaptation F2a   What's Missing?

hasn't got *is missing* Prepositions, street vocabulary	S	7+
		V

Preparation

Make 2 copies of page **V**. One will be page **a** and one page **b**. Use Tippex or Liquid Paper to blank out 5 details on page **a**, such as the wheel of a car or someone's hand, and 5 different details on page **b**. Make enough copies so that half the class have page **a** and half page **b**.

Steps

1   Step 1 as before, explaining that each picture has 5 things missing.
2   Children tell each other in turns what is missing from their picture:

Example   ***The back wheel is missing from the car near the traffic lights.***
             The car near the traffic lights hasn't got a back wheel.

3   Steps 3 and 4 as **F2**.

Adaptation F2b   Two Towns

Names of buildings and adverbs of place: ***near, next to, opposite, on the corner***	S	8+
		R,Y

Preparation

Make 1 copy of page **R** and 1 copy of page **Y**.
Fill in the names of all the buildings on each map, leaving some the same and changing some so that there are differences.

Steps

1   Step 1 as **F2**.
2   Children tell each other in turn where each building is. They tick (✓) the building if it is in the same place. If not, they write the name of their partner's building on the place he describes.
3   Step 3 as **F2**.

F3 Ivan's Day

Telling the time Present simple questions Daily actions	**S**

I

PW

Preparation

Make a copy of page **I** and draw in times on the clocks. There should be 8 times drawn for **C1**, with 8 left blank. Those which are drawn in for **C1** should be blank for **C2**, and vice versa. Decide whether to keep to hours or to add halves, quarters and minutes, according to the age and level of the class.
Make enough copies of page **I** to give 1 copy to each pair. Cut each copy in two.

Steps

1   Put the children into pairs, 1 and 2. Give part **C1** to Child 1 and part **C2** to Child 2.
2   Explain that they have the same pictures, but each of them has the times which are missing on the other child's clock.
3   They must now find the missing times and draw them in.
They will have to ask these sort of questions:
C1 ***What time does Ivan get up?***   C2 ***At 7 o'clock.***
C2 ***What time does he get dressed?***   C1 ***At 7.15.***
C1 ***What time does he catch the bus?***   C2 ***At 7.30.***

Note: Again, you should decide on the type of question form you can expect your class to produce and practise it beforehand.

F4 Buying Presents

Counting money ***What can I buy?***	**S**

Scissors

B

PW

Preparation

— Make copies of page **B**, one for each pair. Cut into parts **C1** and **C2**.
— Tell the class they are going shopping to buy presents. Ask what kinds of things they would buy for Mum, Dad, an older brother, baby sister and a grandmother. Make sure they know the vocabulary on **B**. Check they know the coins on **B** too.

Steps

1   In pairs, give part **C1** to child 1 and part **C2** to child 2. Explain that C1 is the customer and C2 is the shopkeeper. C1 has to buy presents for five members of his family. He has five sets of money cards. He must now add up each of these separately to find five total amounts.
2   While C1 is doing this, C2 must choose a price for each set of three presents from the ones on his sheet. For example, the three presents in set A all cost 53 pence each. C2 should write the price on each present.
3   Each child now cuts along the dotted lines so that C1 has five money cards and C2 has five sets of presents.
4   — C1 chooses a money card, holds it up and says how much it is:
      I have 53p. What can I buy for 53p?
      — C2 looks at the sets of presents and tells C1 the three things he can buy for that amount:
      You can buy a teddy, a box of chocolates or a spanner for 53p.
      — C1 now decides which one he will buy and who it is for:
      Example   ***I'll buy a teddy for my baby sister.***
5   C2 cuts out the present and gives it to C1. C1 gives his money card to C2. C2 puts the two remaining items on one side and C1 writes the name of the present and the price next to the name of the person it is for. He uses his check list for this. (Younger children can just tick the box.)
6   Continue until C1 has bought a suitable present for all five people. If he gets to the end of his money without buying everybody a suitable present, he must choose the most suitable from the remaining items in the shop.
7   At the end of the lesson children tell the class what they have bought and who for.

F5 Cognates

Beginning language awareness in a foreign language and appreciation of cognate words
Making vocabulary acquisition easier

S

7+

CW

Steps

1 Ask children to think of English words which are similar to words in their own language, like **telephone** perhaps. Point out any differences in pronunciation, spelling and meaning. Give a few more examples they may not know.
2 Start a display which children can add to as they learn new words.

F6 Collecting Real English

Beginning language awareness in a foreign language
Appreciating the use of English as an international language
English used in everyday contexts

R

8+

GW

Preparation

Collect tins, packets, advertisements etc. which contain English words, phrases or sentences.

Steps

1 Let children look at the items you have collected and find examples of English. They can cut them from labels, packets or magazines. They can circle the words or use a highlighter pen.
2 You can discuss in L1 the meaning of any which are not too difficult and could be relevant, and also why English is used there.
3 Make a display of these items. Children should add to the display throughout the year. You can examine and discuss the additions at convenient times.
* Older children can find out which English words are used on the most items, and therefore, perhaps, which words are the most useful.

F7 Hide and Seek

Prepositions and adverbs of place: **in the kitchen, under the table**
Questions and short answers: **Yes, I am/No, I'm not**

S

8+

H,F

GW

Preparation

Make a copy of page **H**, add furniture from page **F** and make copies of this, enough for 2 between 3 or 4. Or they can be old copies which the children have already used.

Steps

1 Put the children in groups of 3 (or 4). Give each group 2 copies of page **H**.
2 Child 1 secretly decides where he is going to hide on one copy of **H**, and writes where in his book, such as: **In the dining room, behind the cupboard.** (This prevents cheating.)
3 — Children 2 and 3 must find C1. They can refer to the other copy of **H**. One starts upstairs and the other downstairs.
— They can go in each room only once but they can ask several questions.
Example **I'm in the big bedroom. Are you under the bed?**
If the room and position are in C1's written sentence, C2 wins. If not, C3 asks a question:
I'm in the kitchen. Are you behind the fridge?
C2 and C3 move from room to room searching for C1. If both C2 and C3 have moved out of the room where C1 is hiding, C1 reveals himself and says **I'm the winner. I was hiding in the kitchen, under the table,** for example.

F8 Town Tour

Following directions *Contrasting and describing differences Prepositions and adverbs of place	**L**

9+

R

GW

Preparation

— Make 2 copies of page **R.** On one copy of the map, fill in the names of all the buildings, using page **Y** to help you.
— Decide which places you want the children to write on their maps, and write a tour of the town including these places:

Example *You arrive at the station. Opposite the station you can see a supermarket. Walk down Station Road. The second road on the right is called West Street . . .*

— Take the other copy of the map and alter it, leaving blank only the roads and places you want them to fill in. Make enough copies of this map for 1 between 2 children.

Steps

1 Give each pair a copy of the second map.
2 Tell the children they are going on a tour of a town in England, and they must label the existing buildings as they listen to you reading.
3 Read your tour, stopping to give enough time for the children to label the places.
4 Put children in groups of four. Tell one pair to compare their map with that of the other pair. They can put a circle round any differences.
* With all the class together, each group should describe the differences:

Example **In our picture the pet shop is on the corner, but in your picture it's opposite the flower shop.**

5 You can re-read the text to settle any disagreements.

Extension F8a 10 Questions

Finding out information Asking and answering questions	**S/L**

R,Y

Preparation

Make enough copies for each group of 4 to have 1 copy of page **R** and 1 of page **Y**.

1 Give 1 copy of page **R** to pair **1** in each group, and 1 copy of **Y** to pair **2**. Tell them which buildings they both know so these can be used as references in their questions.
2 Each pair prepares 10 questions (depending on their level and confidence they can prepare more or less than 10) about the buildings **not** marked on their map.

Example **How do you get to the swimming pool from the station?**
    What is opposite the park entrance?
    Is the school near the clock tower?

3 Pair **1** asks 2 questions and marks on the names of the building according to the answers pair **2** gives. Then pair **2** asks 2 questions. The pairs continue asking and answering until they have all the information for their questions.
4 The two pairs now compare the two maps and try to settle differences. Teach the children to talk about these:

Example **You said the hospital was on the <u>left</u> of the school.**

Note: If you decide they should ask fewer questions, for example, 6 questions about 4 or 5 buildings each, fill in 3 or 4 buildings on each map, so they only have 4 or 5 unlabelled buildings each.

F9 Making Graphs: Heights

Language associated with measurement:
How tall are you?
120 centimetres/1 metre 20
Comparatives: **more, most, more than, less than**

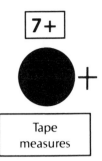

Tape
measures

Q

GW

7+

Preparation

Make copies of page **Q**, 1 for each group.
It is better if you do this activity in two lessons: 1 Gathering the information
2 Representing the information

Steps

1   Ask children how tall they are. For those who know, write the heights on the board against the names. How tall do they think most of the children are? Let them write their guess in their books.

2   Get two children to measure another child. You can ask children to guess the heights of other children by comparison, using sentences like **Pedro is taller than Marie. I think she is about 110 cm.**

3   Children should write on page **Q** the question they are going to ask other children, in this case, **How tall are you?**
Get children to measure each other. Groups of 3–4 are best, each measuring the other in turn. They can record the information on copies of page **Q**. Meanwhile, write all the names of the children on the board.

4   Ask different children for information about other children, using *How tall is _____ ?*
As children tell you how tall they are, write the heights by their names. If there are any differences from step 1, discuss them using **taller/shorter, only 105 cm**, and so on.

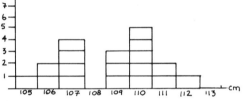

5   Children record all the information either on page **Q** or in their books. This is a good place to break, if you are doing it in two stages.

6   Discuss the results:
Example   **Hans is taller than Leit.**
No children are 108 cm. Eighteen are less than 115 cm.
Explain that they will make graphs to see the information more easily.

7   Give each group a piece of paper and show them how to make a block graph. Alternatively, they can stick on little figures instead of blocks.

8   Discuss the finished product, showing how easily they can see the information.

Adaptation F9a Favourites

Questions: **What's your favourite _____ ?**
What/which _____ do you like best?

Here each group can take a different subject, asking all the others in the class.

Adaptation F9b What did you you do last Saturday?

Asking questions using the past simple tense

Adaptation F9c What will you be when you grow up?

Asking questions using future tense forms

Note: The questionnaire can be adapted

a   to collect information for more children by dividing each of the 12 lines into 2, to give space for 24 answers,

b to ask several questions of 1 person, by swapping over *Question* and *Name*, and writing, instead of the old *Name*, the first part of the question common to all in the space, for example, *Do you like . . .* and below this the rest of the questions, such as *swimming?/orange juice?/school?* etc. The *Answer* section can also be divided into, say, 4 possible answers (*Yes, I love it/Yes, I do/No, I don't/No, I hate it,* or happy and sad faces) which the children can just mark with a cross.

* The questionnaire on page **L** gives another example of use, and can be blanked out and different questions and answers inserted to suit the needs of your class. If you do not want children to write afterwards, cover the bottom half of the page with another copy of the questionnaire, so you have two on a page before you make copies.

F10   Making Sets

Classifying animals into sets, using knowledge of animals Mathematical terms: *set, member*	L

7+

String, large paper

Z/A

GW

Preparation

Make copies of page **Z**, or page **A**, enough for 1 between 3.

Steps

1   Give a copy of page **Z** to each group of 3. Children cut the animals out and tell their partners what they are. Give each group a piece of string 50–80 cm long.
2   Make sure the children know the names of all the animals. If they can, they tie the ends of the string together; if not, they make a loose loop on the table.
3   Remind children they have done sets in their own language and they are going to do the same in English. Ask them to make a set of *animals which have 4 legs*, by placing the cutouts in the loop of string. Check they all agree, by asking how many members are in the set, and to name them.
4   Ask children to make a set of animals which:
    eat meat/don't eat meat/live in hot countries/live in cold countries/live in Africa/can swim/are 1 colour/are bigger than a horse, etc.
5   As far as possible, give each group a different set to make. This should be for display, either on the table, or posted onto a large sheet of paper.
6   Children write the names of all the animals and label the set.

Adaptation F10a   Food Sets

Make copies of page **E**, 1 between 3.
Children make sets of food: *meat/fruit/vegetables/drinks/sweet things/hot food/cold food/vegetarian food,* etc.
Discuss which foods don't fit neatly into the first five sets.

E

Adaptation F10b   Household Objects

Make copies of page **U**, 1 between 3.
Make sure the children know the names of all the objects. Children make sets of *objects which use electricity/are containers (Can you put things in it?)*.
Depending on the language you have covered, ask them to make other sets, such as *things we eat with/drink out of/cook with; things which can be made of metal/plastic/pottery/glass; things we find in the living room/kitchen* etc.

U

Adaptation F10c   Personal Sets

In their books, children draw a circle (Venn diagram) and draw or write in the members of sets which are about themselves: *food I like/games I like to play/my friends/animals I have seen,* etc.

8+

Adaptation F10d Weekly Sets

9+

To practise colours, shapes, textures etc., ask children to bring members of a particular set, and display them for a week. These could be *green/red/white/bright things; round/square/long/triangular things; hard/soft/smooth/rough things; things from trees; things associated with spring/summer/autumn/winter.*

Note: Before starting weekly sets, you can ask children to bring in an object, in a bag, which the others will have to guess by asking questions:

Example   C2   **Is it round?**
           C1   **Yes, it is.**
           C3   **Is it red?**
           C1   **No, it isn't.**
           C2   **What colour is it?**
           C1   **It's white.**
           C3   **Can you see it in a kitchen?**
           C1   **No.**
           C2   **Where can you see it?**
           C1   **In a bathroom.**

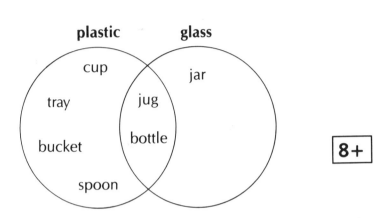

Adaptation F10e Intersections

8+

Children can make two sets, which may intersect:
Example   made of plastic, made of glass.

F11 What's Wrong?

> Listening for detail, pointing out mistakes:
>   **That's wrong. You said _____ but _____ .**

L   8+

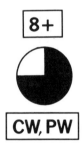

CW, PW

The class and pair activities can be done as separate lessons.

Preparation

1   Write a few lines about one of the animals children have learned about, but include 4 deliberate mistakes:
Example   *Elephants live in India and America. The African elephant is bigger than the Indian elephant. Elephants can weigh twenty tonnes. They eat grass, leaves, rabbits and deer. They have big ears and a long nose called a tusk.*
This is your version which the children will not see.
2   On a sheet of A4 paper write 2 similar descriptions for 2 other animals, neat enough for children to read. On the same sheet write the correct facts for both. Make enough copies for 1 between 2 and cut into 4 sections.

Steps

1   — Tell the class to think of what they know about elephants. (If you feel they do not know enough to spot the 4 mistakes, you can put a complete correct version of your elephant passage on the board, and read the incorrect passage.)
     — Tell them you will read some information about elephants twice. The first time they must just listen.
     — Read your version once. Now tell them they must put up their hand when they hear something wrong.
     — Read again. When a hand goes up, ask *What's wrong?*
     — Encourage children to point out the wrong words, not just give the correct version:
       Example   **You said elephants live in America, but they live in Africa.**
     — Continue until all the mistakes have been spotted, if necessary reading a third time.

2 Ask if any child can tell the rest of the class about elephants, and let him do so.

3 Tell the children they are going to do the same in pairs with different animals. Give child 1 a copy of the faulty description and Child 2 some true facts. Explain that C1 will read, and C2 should interrupt saying *That's wrong. You said _____ but _____ .*

4 As each pair finishes, give C2 the second description and C1 the true facts, and repeat as in step 3.

5 Ask if any children can tell the class about these two animals, or any others.

Extension F11a Story-telling

Do the same with any stories the children have read and heard. Write a summary with 4–6 mistakes. You will need two stories if they do it in pairs. You don't need to write the correct version — rely on the children's memory.

In this version, older children may be able to tell stories with their own deliberate mistakes.

Extension F11b Subjects

Do the same with anything they have learned about in your class or in any other subject — history, geography, science.

F12-F15 Making Sense of Things

Some of the activities will contain new vocabulary, but you can use them for teaching the new words, rather than for practice. Start collecting the items well in advance.

F12 A Bag of Secrets

> Describing objects
> Adjectives of shape, size, texture (feel):
> **round, square, thin, thick, pointed; rough, smooth**

S 9+

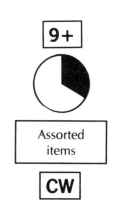

Assorted items

CW

Preparation

Collect about 20 items such as beads, buttons, marbles, coins, rings, cotton reels, different fabrics, sandpaper. Put them in a box or bag which children can put a hand in, but cannot see inside — a cotton bag tied with string is ideal.

Steps

1 One child puts a hand in the bag and describes what one of the items feels like:
Example *It's round and flat, it's big, it's quite smooth.* The child should not name it.

2 Other children try to guess what it is from the description. The first child says which guess he thinks is correct, then takes out the item to see if they are right.

3 Ask the class for a good description of the item, prompting them where necessary.

4 Other children take turns to feel an object.

F13 Have a Taste

> Adjectives of taste and texture:
> **sweet, bitter, sour, hot, spicy, salty, hard, soft, lumpy, sticky, runny, thick, solid, chewy**

S 9+

Containers and things to taste

CW

Preparation

Prepare a number of containers (yogurt pots are ideal) each containing a different taste, such as yogurt, curry, lemon, orange, peanut butter, Marmite etc. You will need a number of teaspoons, or better, plastic coffee stirrers or ice cream spoons.

Note: Send a note home to parents a week before you do this activity to ask if the child has any health problems such as allergies, diabetes etc. which would stop them tasting the food.

Steps

1 Without letting the children see what it is, put a small amount of one food on the tongues of several children. Ask them to describe the taste and also the texture, **without** naming it.
2 Let the other children try to guess what it is. Children who have tasted it say which guess they think is right.
3 Repeat with other children and other tastes.
4 Finally children name the items and make a good description of each one.

Extension F13a

Comparatives and superlatives

Let children taste two or more items and compare which is hotter, sweeter, smoother etc.

F14 How Does It Smell?

> Adjectives of smell: *mild, faint, strong, sweet, nasty, nice*
> *It smells like flowers,* etc.

Containers and things to smell

Preparation

Prepare some small corked bottles and fill them with solids and liquids with different smells, such as herbs, spices, crushed garlic, coffee, cheese, vinegar, perfumes, eau de Cologne. If you have enough bottles, children can do the activity in groups.

Steps

Let children pass round a bottle and smell the contents. Help them to describe the smell and guess the contents.

Extension F14a

> Comparatives and superlatives   S

Let children smell two or more items and compare which is stronger, nicer, sweeter, milder etc.

F15 Can You Hear?

> Verbs of sound: *clapping, whispering*
> Onomatopoeic verbs/nouns: *bang, splash, hiss*
> Present participle: *a door creaking, pouring water*
> *Adjectives of sound: *mysterious, relaxing, noisy, musical*

Steps

1 Ask children to tell you some of the sounds you can hear at home (a door closing, water pouring, cars driving past).
2 Ask them to tell you and show you some of the sounds you can make with your body (clapping, stamping feet, clicking fingers, slapping your knee, swallowing, whispering, whistling).
3 Give examples of some words which sound like what they mean (onomatopoeia). Ask children to think of more (*bump, bang, slam, crash, splash, buzz, hiss, moo, miaow, cuckoo*). They can compare these with words in their own language.
4 Ask one child to go behind the others if possible, and make a noise. You can whisper to him to be, for example, a lion roaring, a door creaking. Other children try to guess what sound he is making.
* If you have a cassette of sound effects, or can make one, you can ask children to describe the sound, and say what they think it is. You could include a clock ticking, water running, a tap dripping, a bell ringing, wood breaking, a knife scraping.

Section G Songs, Rhymes and Chants

Suggested procedure for all activities used without music:
1   You say the rhyme first, then emphasise the rhythm, saying *da, da, da* instead of the syllables.
2   Get the students to copy you, first with the rhythm, then adding words. Work through it, repeating 2 or more words at a time, depending on what they can manage.
3   Go through one line at a time, and when children are confident, do the whole activity straight through. G6-G10 may be better divided over two lessons.

G1 Food Train — Chant

Practising English rhythm and food collocations	S

6–10

CW

This should sound like a train getting faster and finally blowing its whistle. Repeat each line, except the last, four times.

What is the train bringing?

Bacon and eggs	x 4	Rhythm
Apples and pears	x 4	
Bread and butter	x 4	
Plums and custard	x 4	
Cheese and biscuits	x 4	
Fish and chips	x 4	
Chocolate cake	x 4	
Ice cream	x 4	

Soooooooooooooooooooup!

G2 Who Stole The Cake? — Chant

Practising quick response in a repeated dialogue using English sentence rhythm	S

6+

CW

Everyone: ***Who stole the cake from the baker's shop?***

Teacher points to Marie, who stands up and gives another child's name.

Marie: ***Tony stole the cake from the baker's shop.***

Tony: ***Who, me?***

Everyone: ***Yes, you.***

Tony: ***Not me.***

Everyone: ***Then who?***

Tony: ***Sophie stole the cake from the baker's shop.***

Sophie: ***Who, me?***

Everyone: ***Yes, you.*** etc.

Extension G2a

Use a different accusation:

Who stole an apple from the greengrocer's shop?

Who took the chalk from the teacher's room?

G3 Counting-out Rhymes

Practising English rhythm	S

6+

GW

These are used when selecting children for teams, to do an activity, to be a leader etc. Point to a child at each of the given marks. The child who is pointed to on the last marked syllable is 'out'. You will find that children will learn them and use them outside school. To practise in class, children see who is left from a group of 4 or 5.

1 Skip, Dip, Sky Blue, who's IT? Not you,
   Not because you're dirty, not because you're clean,
   My Mum says you're a silly old bean, so OUT you go.

2 One, two, three, four, five, six, seven, all good children go to heaven,
   A penny on the railway, twopence on the sea,
   Threepence on an aeroplane, and OUT goes she/he.

3 Eeny meeny miney mo, catch a spider on your toe,
   If it tickles, let it go, eeny meeny miney mo.

G4 Two Hungry Crocodiles — Action rhyme

Adjectives, verbs and adverbs of place	S

6–9

CW

Two hungry crocodiles waiting at the gate	(With both hands in front, make
One called Sally, one called Kate	snapping actions of crocodile's jaws)
Go away Sally	(Put right arm behind)
Go away Kate	(Put left arm behind)
Come back Sally	(Bring right arm back)
Come back Kate	(Bring left arm back)

Extension G4a

Change the rhyme by substituting other animals, verbs or places:

Two pretty parrots sitting on the gate . . . Fly away Sally, fly away Kate

Two furry tigers sitting by the gate . . . Run away Sally, run away Kate

Two lazy pussy cats lying on the chair, One called Larry, one called Claire

Note: You can use the ideas in activity **D6**, **Story-telling with Puppets**, to make visuals of the animals and birds.

G5 I Can Waggle My Fingers — Action rhyme

Parts of the body and associated verbs	S

6+

CW

I can . . . waggle my fingers, stand on my toes, touch my ears and wrinkle my nose,
   lift my elbow, bend my wrist, stick out my thumb and shake my fist,
   smack my leg, wiggle my hips, pat my cheeks and close my lips. (pause)
I can . . . touch my ankles, bend my knee, cover my eyes — now I can't see.

Alternative G5a

Use **touch** instead of the verbs given, for a simpler version.

G6 Good Morning

Practising days of the week
Greetings

CW/PW

1 Teach the song if you can use a musical instrument to play the music, otherwise teach it as a chant, taking the rhythm from the stress pattern marked above the words.

2 Practise it using all the days of the week. Go through the first verse 2–4 words at a time, repeating them as often as necessary. Divide the song over 2–3 lessons if you prefer.

3 When they are more confident, you can divide the class into 2 or into pairs facing each other:

A *Good morning, good morning.*
How do you do?

B *Good morning, good morning.*
How do you do?

A *Today it is Monday.*

B *Yes, it is Monday.*

A *Can you play with me?*

B *Yes, I can play with you.* etc.

Words — Jane Pettigrew
Music — Geoffrey Tyler

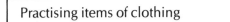

* Use other days of the week in following verses.

G7 What Shall I Wear?

Practising items of clothing

CW/PW

1 Teach the song or chant, as in **G6**, changing the items of clothing verse by verse.

2 The children can pretend to put on the various clothes, miming, for example, putting on and buttoning up a shirt. You can ask individual children to sing the lines:

Put on your shirt,
Put on your shirt,
This is what you should wear today.

You can get them to choose the item they will sing.

3 It can also be done in pairs, **A** speaking his 3 lines, then **B**:

A *What shall I wear?*
What shall I wear?
What shall I wear to school today?

B *Put on your shirt,*
Put on your shirt,
This is what you should wear today. etc.

Words — Jane Pettigrew
Music — Geoffrey Tyler

G8 Ten Green Frogs

| Practising numbers (any range of numbers, not just 1–10) | S | 6–9 |

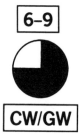

CW/GW

1 Teach the song or chant, as in **G6.**
2 Arrange the children in groups of 10. They can stand or squat like frogs on chairs, benches, cushions, or in a circle. One by one they jump off 'into the water' as the verses progress.

Ten green frogs eating ten fat flies,

Sat by a pool on a hot summer's day,

One finished his fly and jumped in the pool,

Hoping to swim in the water cool,

And then there were nine green frogs.

Nine green frogs eating nine fat flies, etc.

Words — Jane Pettigrew
Music — Geoffrey Tyler

G9 This Is The Way

| Present simple tense
Everyday verbs of action
Times of the day | S | 6+ |

CW/GW

1 Teach the song or chant, with the class miming the actions verse by verse.
2 You can get the children to suggest some of the actions. At other times you sing the song you can get the children to change the pronouns: . . . **we wash our hands;** . . . **she washes her hands** etc.

This is the way I wash my hands,   *This is the way I brush my teeth,*

Wash my hands, wash my hands,   *Brush my teeth, brush my teeth,*

This is the way I wash my hands,   *This is the way I brush my teeth,*

At six o'clock in the morning.   *At six o'clock in the morning.*

Other actions: **comb my hair; tie my shoes; eat my breakfast; drink my milk;**
        wash the dishes; sweep the floor; cook the dinner; lay the table;
        open the door; catch a ball; write my name; go to sleep (sing slowly).

Change the times to appropriate times of the day.

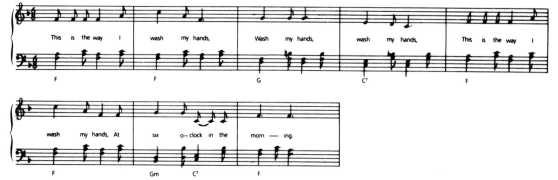

G10 Old MacDonald Had a Farm

Names of animals and animal noises

S

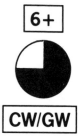

CW/GW

1 Teach the song or chant, as in **G6**.
2 Choose individuals or pairs of children to be the various animals and make the noises.
Each time a verse is sung, one more animal is added. Each animal makes its sound in turn.
The quicker it is done, the more fun it is.

Note: The letters **E, I** and **O** are pronounced the same as they are in the alphabet.

Old MacDonald had a farm, E, I, E, I, O,

And on that farm he had a dog, E, I, E, I, O,

With a woof woof here and a woof woof there,

Here a woof, there a woof, everywhere a woof woof,

Old MacDonald had a farm, E, I, E, I, O.

Old MacDonald had a farm, E, I, E, I, O,

And on that farm he had some cows, E, I, E, I, O,

With a moo moo here and a moo moo there,

Here a moo, there a moo, everywhere a moo moo,

Old MacDonald had a farm, E, I, E, I, O, etc.

Repeat with ducks (***quack, quack***), hens (***cluck, cluck***), cats (***miaow, miaow***), pigs (***oink, oink***), sheep (***baa, baa***), horses (***neigh, neigh***), donkeys (***ee-ore, ee-ore***).

Section H Games, Puzzles and Quizzes

H1 Jaws

Reinforcing spelling patterns and letter combinations	W

Children prefer this to the traditional version, *Hangman.*

Steps

1   Draw 12 steps on the board. Draw a boy or girl (give a name, say, Chico) on the top step. Draw waves and the fin of a shark at the bottom. Or you can use a cutout figure from page **P** and cut out a shark (page **D** and add a fin), and use sticky tack so they can be moved.

2   Think of a word all the children know and draw a dash for each letter.

3   Ask children to suggest a letter. If the letter occurs in the word, write it on the correct dash. If it does not occur, write the letter at the side and move Chico down a step.

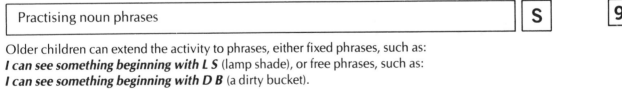

4   The children have to guess all the letters before Chico falls into the sea and is eaten by the shark. Use language to dramatise the game, for example *The shark's going to get him. Poor Chico!* If Chico is getting eaten rather too often, he can occasionally be rescued by helicopter!

5   Children do the game in groups, one child choosing the word in turn. They should not use dictionaries — it should be a word most children know.

H2 I Can See

Practising the alphabet and vocabulary	S

Steps

1   One child looks around the room and says, for example, ***I can see something beginning with*** **W.** The others have to guess what it is, saying, ***Is it a*** _____? ***Is it the*** _____? When someone has guessed what it is, another child has a turn.

2   When children have the idea, they play in pairs or small groups. Children can also use the photocopiable pages of this book, or pictures or posters, for example, of a seaside scene.

Extension H2a

Practising noun phrases	S

| 9+ |

Older children can extend the activity to phrases, either fixed phrases, such as:
I can see something beginning with L S (lamp shade), or free phrases, such as:
I can see something beginning with D B (a dirty bucket).

Adaptation H2b

Asking questions	S

| 9+ |
| A4 paper |

Steps

1   Give a sheet of A4 paper to each child of the pair or group. One child draws a picture without others seeing and says, ***I'm drawing something beginning with*** _____ .

2   The others have to guess what he is drawing by asking, ***Does it have legs? Is it an animal? Can I eat it?*** etc. When someone has guessed what it is, another child has a turn.

H3 Word Snap

Building vocabulary
Matching related items

S

6+

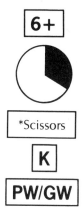

*Scissors

K

PW/GW

Preparation

Make copies of page **K**, one between 2–4 children. Cut out the pictures to make a pack of 32 cards, or get the children to cut out the pictures. Check the pictures and preteach any new vocabulary.

Steps

1   One child shuffles and places the cards in rows without looking at them. They should have the 32 cards upside down in front of them. In turn, each child turns up one card. It remains face up.
2   When a child sees two matching cards he calls out the names, for example, ***table and chair***, and collects the pair. The child with most pairs wins.

Adaptation H3a Picture Pelmanism

Use the same cards as in **H3.**
The game can be played by 2, 3 or 4 children. Children place the cards randomly upside down on the table. In turn, each child turns over two cards. If they match, he says what they are and collects them. He can then have another turn. If they do not match, he turns them face down again in exactly the same place, and the next child has a turn. The child with the most pairs wins.

Adaptation H3b Picture Dominoes

Make copies of page **K**, one for each pair. Cut the sheet into 16 pairs of pictures, 2 pictures on each card, for example, a car and a cup.
Each child takes 8 dominoes. C1 puts a domino on the table, face up. C2 must place a matching picture on either end of C1's domino, naming the pair that match. If he can't, he misses a turn. The first child to put all his dominoes out is the winner.

PW

H4 Food Bingo

Classifying food and drink

L

6+

E

IW

Preparation

Make copies of page **E**, 1 between 2. Cut the pages into 8 strips, with 4 pictures on each strip. Shuffle the strips to mix them up.

Steps

1   Give 4 strips to each child, making sure no child has two the same. If they have, get them to swap the strip with a child near them.
2   Tell children they must cross off one item of the type you will call out:
    Example   *Cross out your favourite food from those you can see.*
              Cross out 1 drink; 1 vegetable; 1 fruit; 1 meat;
              something sweet; something hot; another fruit . . . etc.
    Keep a list of what you have called.

3   The first child to cross out 4 pictures on one strip is the winner. Check they are correct. He should say what his 4 items were:
    Example   ***My favourite food is _____ . The drink is _____ .***
    Or he can simply say the name of the item and you can ask the class: *Is that a drink? What is it?* to check against your list.
4   You can use the same strips to play again if you use pencils first, then pencils or pens of different colours. Children should exchange strips with others each time.
Note: You can make variations by using other pages, eg C, N, O, U, A/Z, but decide on simple definitions beforehand. This game can be simplified by calling out only the name of the items.

H5 Space Wars

Practising numbers and letters Vocabulary of spacecraft	S

7+

X

PW

Preparation

One 1 copy of page **X** write letters A-J across the top and 1-10 down one side of each box (see **A1**)
Make copies of page **X**, so that each child has a 10 x 10 box square. Go over the items of space vocabulary with the children.

Steps

1   Give a copy of the box square to each child and put them in pairs. Each child now places his spacecraft on the grid, one to a square. He should use these abbreviations:

Each child is allowed 2 Satellite Stations	SS	5 Star Cruisers	SC
3 Rocket Transports	RT	2 Space Battleships	SB
He should also place 2 Space Mines	SM	1 Black Hole	BH

2   The children take it in turns to call out a letter and a number:
   Example   C1 **_B2_**   C2 **_A Star Cruiser_**
   — If that square on Child 2's paper is blank, C1 puts a cross in the top left corner of his square so that he doesn't call the same square twice.
   — If C2's square contains an SS, SC, RT, or SB, then it is hit and destroyed. C2 puts a cross through the whole square and C1 writes SS (etc.) in the top left corner on his sheet.
3   C2 now calls a letter and a number.
4   If a child hits a Satellite Station (SS), he gets two extra turns. If he hits a Space Mine (SM), he loses two turns. If he hits a Black Hole (BH), he loses the game immediately.
5   The game is over as soon as one child has destroyed all the spacecraft of his partner, or if one child hits a Black Hole.

Note: you may choose to use alternatives to spacecraft. For example _Cats and Mice, Giants and Demons._

H6 Treasure Hunt

Revision: answering questions about English	L/W

6+

1 die,
counters

G

CW

This will add colour and interest to any test or quiz-like activity. It is flexible so you can use it more than once with the same class. It follows the usual board game pattern: children start on square 1 and move forward in a race to reach the treasure.

Preparation

— Make copies of page **G**, 1 between 2 children. Prepare a list of 20-30 questions (see example).
— Each child needs a button, a coin or a coloured piece of paper to move as a counter. Two children play on one page.

Steps

1   Explain the game to the children. Check that they understand what they must do if they land on the special squares — 5, 9, 14, 17, 20, 26 and 30.
2   Tell them you are going to throw a die. Whichever number comes up will be the number they can move forward if they get your question right. So if you throw a 3, all the children who get the answer right will move 3 squares.
3   Ask a question and tell the children to write down the answer. See the examples below. Elicit the correct answer and write it on the board. All the children with the right answer move their figures forward. Those who are wrong stay where they are.
4   Ask more questions until the game ends. This is when:
   a) one or more children reach the treasure, or
   b) you have finished asking a certain number of questions, so the child or children nearest the treasure are the winners.

Note: An alternative to throwing a die is for you to call out a number according to the level of difficulty.

Example questions (but you can use almost any questions and adapt the level).

Spelling: *How do you spell cat?*

Odd Word Out: *Which is the odd word out? Apple, pear, lemonade, banana.*

Opposites: *What is the opposite of day?*

Sentence completion: *A baby cat is called a _____ .*

Grammar: *What is the past of do?*
 We say I am but she _____ ?

General: *Which day of the week comes after Wednesday?*

H7 I Went To Market (ABC Version)

Reinforcing vocabulary	S

8+

CW

Steps

1 Tell the children they are going to play a game to make them think of as many words as possible. Tell them to stand up.

2 Say *I went to market and I bought an apple*.
 Point to the first child (e.g. Maria) and say *Maria went to market and bought an apple and a brush*.
 Get Maria to repeat, saying **I went . . .**
 Get a second child to say, **I went to market and bought an apple, a brush and a c . . .** etc.

3 If a child cannot remember an item, or think of a word for his letter, he sits down. If you reach the end of the class, return to the first child. If you reach **z** start at **a** again. It is useful to have a picture of a xylophone or a quince to help the unlucky child who gets **x** or **q**, or omit these letters altogether. The winner is the last child left.

Adaptation H7a I went to (somewhere in your country) . . .

Adaptation H7b Single letter version

9+

GW

In groups of 4–6, give each group a different letter. The students must choose items beginning with that letter. In this version it is easier to get a winner, with one child left at the end.

H8 Odd Word Out

Classifying items *all _____ except _____ , all _____ but _____ .*	S

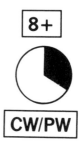

8+

CW/PW

Note: If children have done this activity in their own language, start with **H8a**.

1 Write or draw 5 items on the board, 4 of which belong to one category and 1 which does not, such as *chair, table, car, bed, desk.*

2 Ask children which one is different and why. Accept any sensible suggestion and if necessary help children express it:
 Example **They are all furniture except the car.**
 You can see them all in a house but you can't see a car in a house.
 or simply, **You can't see a car in a house.**

3 Repeat with other items until children have got the idea. They can now invent their own and try it out on a partner.

Extension H8a

In later lessons you can make the connections less obvious, and finally ambiguous, so that there can be more than one answer and they lead to more discussion:
 Example T *penguin, eagle, crow, bat, pigeon.*
  C1 **They can all fly except the penguin.**
  C2 **They are all birds except the bat.**

Extension H8b

As you cover further language points, use the activity as extra practice:

Example   *They are all **made of** paper except the cassette.*
            *They are all **used for** cutting except the spoon.*

H9 Word Draughts

Consolidating __s, __es and __ies plural endings
Language for games: ***It's your turn***
                    You can't go there

| R | 8+ |

*Scissors

W

PW

Preparation

Make copies of page **W**, 1 for each pair. Cut out the black and white counters, or ask the children to do it.

Steps

1   One player has white squares and counters, the other has black. Each player places their 8 counters on the singular squares of the same colour. (The idea is to move to the other side of the board to the plural squares.)
2   Each player moves diagonally in any direction, one square at a time, but they may jump over their opponent's pieces horizontally or vertically onto their own colour.
3   The winner is the first player to cover all their plural squares with singular counters of the same word.

H10 Funny Meals

Stating preferences: ***I prefer _____ to _____***
I like _____ better than _____
Superlatives: ***nicest, strangest, silliest***

| S | 6–11 |

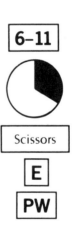

Scissors

E

PW

Preparation

Make copies of page **E**, enough for one between 8. Cut them in half.
You can cut each half into 16 cards, or ask each group to cut theirs.

Steps

1   Put children in groups of four. Give each group a half sheet of page **E** to cut out, or the 16 cards. Each pair of adjoining groups should have a different set. You can tell the children they are going to make a funny packed lunch.
2   The cards are shuffled and placed in a pile, face down. The first child takes two cards. He must say which food he prefers and return one card to the centre, face up:
    Example   ***I prefer cheese to carrots.***
                I like tea better than ice cream.
3   The next child takes the card which is face up **and** the top card of the pile, says which he prefers, and discards one. The game continues until each child has 4 assorted foods, which they then describe to the others:
    Example   ***I've got an apple, some milk, an ice cream and some tea for my packed lunch.***
    They can decide which is the nicest and which is the strangest meal.
*   Each group can then describe the four meals to the adjoining group, who describe their four meals. The combined group then decides which is the nicest/strangest/silliest out of the eight meals.

H11 Snakes and Ladders

Games language: ***It's your/my turn***
You can go up the ladder
You must go down the snake

Numbers 1–100

*Sentences starting ***If . . .***

*****went up, fell down, the most***

Dice, counters, coloured pencils

X

PW

8+

Preparation

Make copies of page **X** enough for each pair to have one 10 x 10 square.

Steps

1 Give out a box square to each pair. Children write numbers 1–100 in alternate directions from the bottom left corner. You can tell Child 1 to write 1–10 from left to right, Child 2 to write 11–20 from right to left:

```
21 22
20 19 18 17 16 15 14 13 12 11
 1  2  3  4  5  6  7  8  9 10          etc.
```

2 Tell children to draw 8 ladders and 8 snakes of different lengths, starting and finishing on different squares. If necessary show them a snakes and ladders board. If you cannot get dice, children can scrape the paint off a six-sided pencil and mark the sides 1 to 6. They need a counter each (plastic discs, nuts or coins). They can colour the top and bottom squares of each snake and ladder.

3 Ask the children to draw a small snake and a small ladder in their books and to keep a count of how many times they fall down the snakes and climb up the ladders.

4 Children can now play the game. See **Rules** below.

* For extra language practice you can tell them that before they can move they have to say a sentence starting ***If . . .***
Example   ***If I get a 3, I'll fall down the ladder.***
When they have finished, they can play again, or do Extension **a** as a written exercise.

5 Ask which children fell down no/1/2/3 (etc.) snakes. Find out who fell down the most snakes and climbed up the most ladders.

* Children write or copy sentences in their books recording this information, with sentences about themselves and their partners:
Examples   ***I fell down 9 snakes.***
Sara fell down the most snakes, she fell down 21 times

RULES

• Take turns to throw the dice and move that number. • If you land at the foot of a ladder, go straight to the top. • If you land on a snake's head, go down to the tail. • The first to reach 100 wins.

Extension H11a Suppose

Suppose you . . .
If clauses

S

10+

CW

Steps

1 Say to the children *Suppose you are on square number 21. If you a throw a 4, where will you land?* Most will answer 25. *Who will land on a different number?* (A child who has the end of a snake or ladder on square 25.)

2 Repeat with 3 or 4 more examples.

3 Get the children to ask each other ***Suppose . . . If . . .*** questions. You can help them with an outline sentence on the board:
Suppose you . . . . If you . . . , where will you land?

Note: it should not be necessary to pre-teach **land.**

H12 Multiplication Square

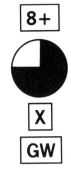

Mathematical language: *times/multiplied by* **What is three times three?**	S

Preparation

Make copies of page **X**, so that each child has a 10 x 10 box square.

Steps

1   Children should write numbers 1–10 across the top
    and down the side of their box square. Alternatively,
    you can make a master copy before photocopying,
    with 1–10 already written on.
2   If they don't know how to make a table square, show
    them how. They multiply the number at the top of a
    column by the number at the side and write the
    answer in the box where they meet.
3   Check their answers by writing up a table on the
    board and eliciting the answers from them. Or go
    round the class checking as the childen fill in their
    grids.
4   Put children in groups of 4. One child is the question
    master:

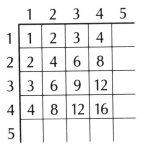

Example   **What is six times three?**
          What is four multiplied by eight? etc.

The others look at the square where a 6 and a 3 meet. The first child to give the correct answer
gets 1 point.
Each child keeps his own score, which the question master checks. The winner is the first child
to get 10 right answers.
Children take it in turns to be the question master.

Adaptation H12a Division Square

Mathematical language: *into, divided by*	S

Steps

Use the same square, but children ask:
Example   **What's five into forty-five?**
          What's sixty-three divided by seven?
This time they look down the '5' column until they get to 45, then they look across to the side to see
the answer.

Note: Children can do **H12a** and **H12b** without the square, but children who are weak in
Mathematics will not get much practice.

Extension H12b Right or Wrong

Mathematical language (see H12 and H12a): *equal(s), is, are, goes*	S

Steps

1   Use the same square as in **H12.** In groups of 4, one child says:
    Example   **Four times eight is twenty-seven.**
              Five sixes are thirty.
              Seventy-two divided by nine is eight etc.
2   The other children call, **Right!** or **Wrong!**
    The first child to call the correct response has the next chance to make up a sum and gets
    1 point. The first child to get 5 points is the winner.

H13 Who Lives Where?

Reading comprehension and deduction from given information Prepositions	R

The suitability of this activity depends entirely on the class and the teacher's decision to adapt where necessary.

Steps

1 Draw five houses on the board and ask children to do the same on paper. While they are doing this, write:
Maria lives next to Tony.
Ben lives between Tony and Ali.
Farah lives in the house on the left, next to Maria.
Who lives where?
To make it easier, you can write the sentences in an easier order (Farah . . . , Maria . . . , Ben . . . , Who . . . ?).

2 If you wish, children can copy this. In pairs they decide who lives where and write the names in each house. If they need help, read one sentence at a time and ask *Do you know where _____ lives?* after each one.

3 They check with a nearby pair to see if they have the same result.

Answer: (in order) Farah, Maria, Tony, Ben, Ali.

Extension H13a

Use the same situation but change the information. Check that only 1 answer is possible.

Example   *Tony lives in the house in the middle.*
                Ben lives next to Ali.
                Ali lives in the house on the right.
                Maria lives between Farah and Tony.
Answer: (in order) Farah, Maria, Tony, Ben, Ali.

Extension H13b

Change the number involved. For example, draw 4 houses on one side of a street and 4 on the other, and number them 1 2 3 4
                        8 7 6 5

David lives in number 5.
Ben lives between Maria and David.
Tony lives opposite Maria.
Sven lives between Tony and Roland.
Farah lives next to Maria and opposite Ali.
Where does Roland live?
Answer: Roland lives in number 4.

Extension H13c

Change the situations:
Dogs living in kennels: horses in stables; animals in cages in a zoo; children sitting round a table (useful for **opposite**); people in a queue (only the first 3 can get on the bus — who are they?)
Example   Draw a bus and 5 people. Say that only 3 people can get on the bus, and point to the first 3 people. While the children draw them, write:
                Mr Green is behind Mrs Brown.
                Mr White is between Mr Green and Mr Black.
                Mrs Grey is in front of Mrs Brown.
                Who can get on the bus?
Answer: Mrs Grey, Mrs Brown and Mr Green.

H14 How Long Are They?

Reading comprehension and deduction
Comparisons: *longer/shorter than*   **R**

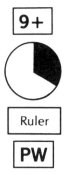

9+

Ruler

PW

Steps

1   Draw four cars on the board and give them four colours. Write, for example:
    The blue car is 3.20 metres long.
    The green car is 20 cm longer than the red car.
    The red car is half a metre shorter than the blue car.
    The white car is 10 cm shorter than the green car.
2   Children work out in pairs how long each car is, and draw them in order, longest first.
    They should check their results with another pair.
Answer: blue = 3.20m, red = 2.70m, green = 2.90m, white = 2.80m.

Adaptation H14a

Comparisons of other adjectives:
   taller, shorter, heavier, lighter, more expensive, cheaper   **R**

Bring in items to help, so that there is something visual, if you do this without writing down
sentences. Use heights of children, weights of bags of fruit, prices of furniture/cars.

H15 Pictograms

Practising English vocabulary and spelling   **W**

8+

PW

Steps

1   As an example, give the class a pictogram to solve, for example:

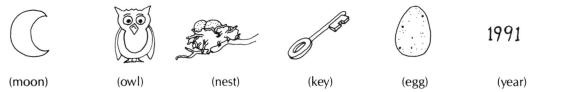

(moon)   (owl)   (nest)   (key)   (egg)   (year)

Tell them the first letter of each picture will spell a new word. **(monkey)**
*   Children make their own pictogram and ask another pair to solve it.

H16 What Does it Mean?

Revising vocabulary, spelling practice   **L**

8+

TW

Steps

1   Divide the class into 2 or 3 teams.
2   Choose a word (for example, from words recently learned). Tell the children the first letter and
    its meaning:
    Example   *I'm thinking of an animal beginning with **c**.* (cat)
    Other clues can be given if necessary:
    Example   *It has three letters. It is small, has a tail, and can live with us at home.*
       or   *Something beginning with **g**. We wear them in winter. We wear them to keep warm.*
            The word has six letters. We wear them on our hands. (gloves)
3   The first child to put up his hand and give the correct answer scores a point for his team. If he is
    wrong then his team loses one point. You can give a bonus point if the same child can also spell
    the word.

Note: The above game can also be played using dictionaries.

Contents of Photocopiable Section

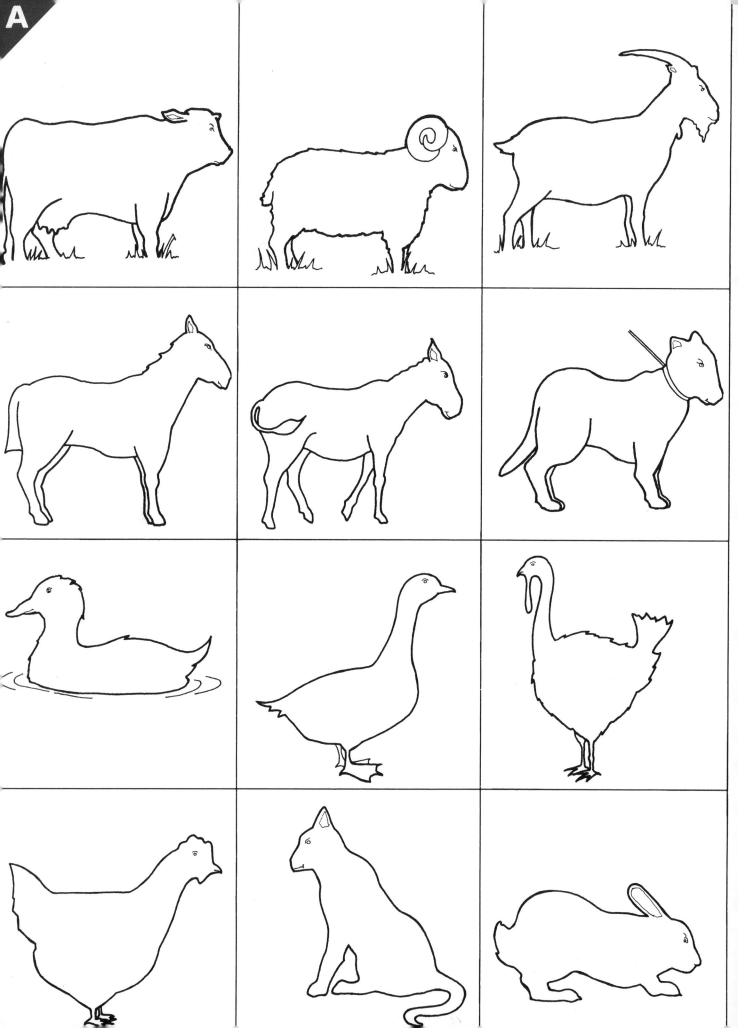

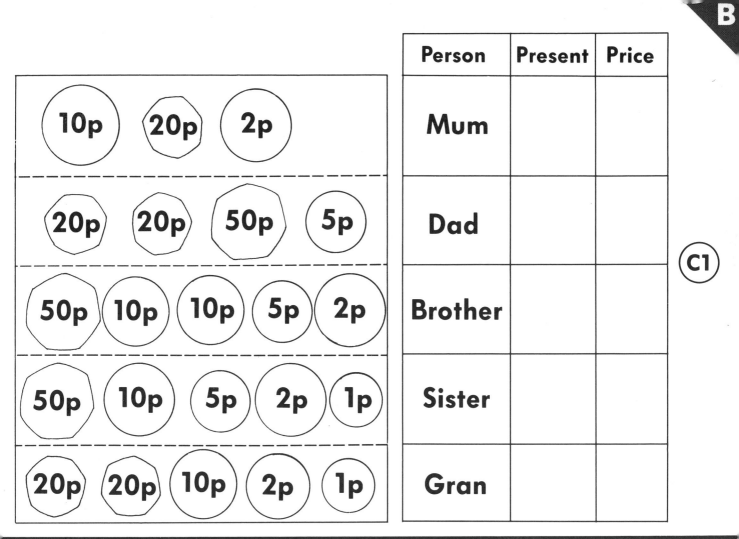

Person	Present	Price
Mum		
Dad		
Brother		
Sister		
Gran		

C1

Prices to put on the pictures				
32p	95p	77p	53p	68p

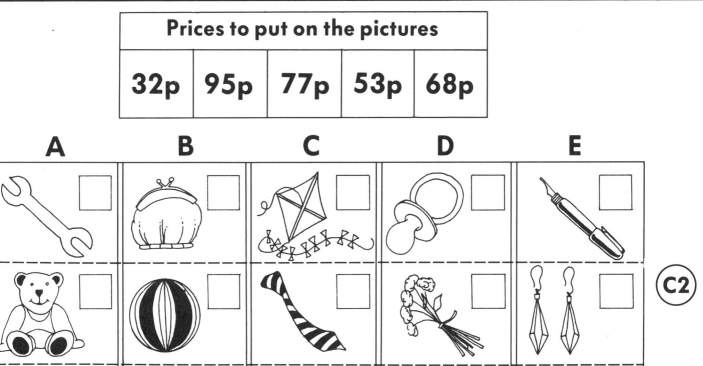

A B C D E

C2

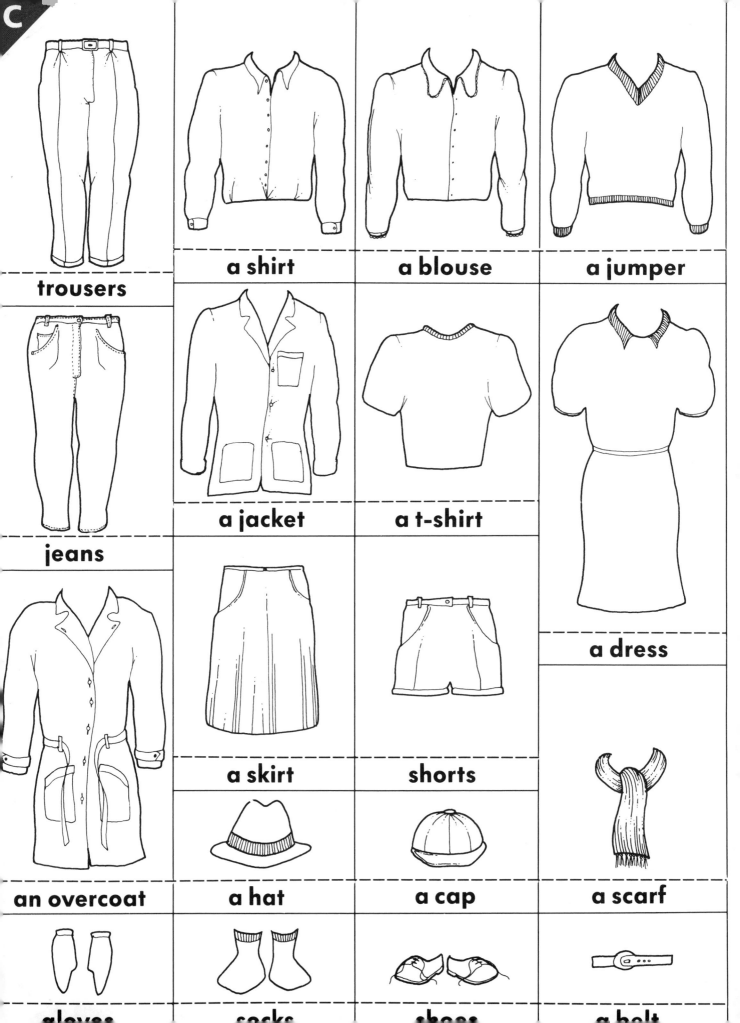

trousers

a shirt

a blouse

a jumper

jeans

a jacket

a t-shirt

a skirt

shorts

a dress

an overcoat

a hat

a cap

a scarf

gloves

socks

shoes

a belt

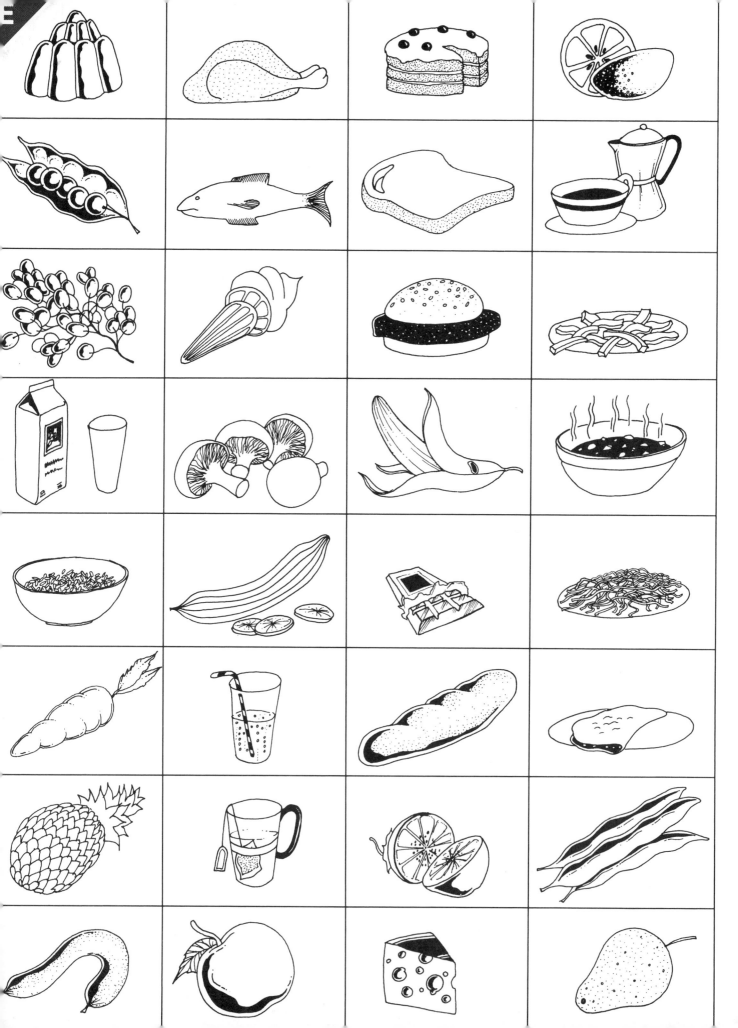

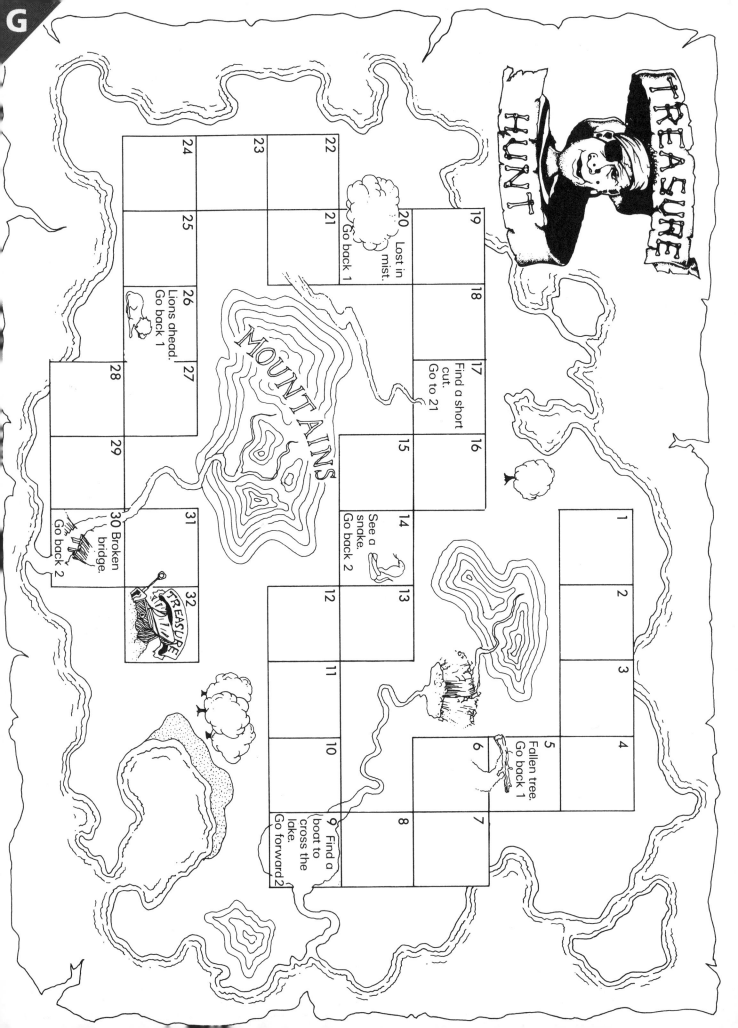

TREASURE HUNT

1

2

3

4

5 Fallen tree. Go back 1

6

7

8

9 Find a boat to cross the lake. Go forward 2

10

11

12

13

14 See a snake. Go back 2

15

16

17 Find a short cut. Go to 21

18

19

20 Lost in mist. Go back 1

21

22

23

24

25

26 Lions ahead. Go back 1

27

28

29

30 Broken bridge. Go back 2

31

32 TREASURE

MOUNTAINS

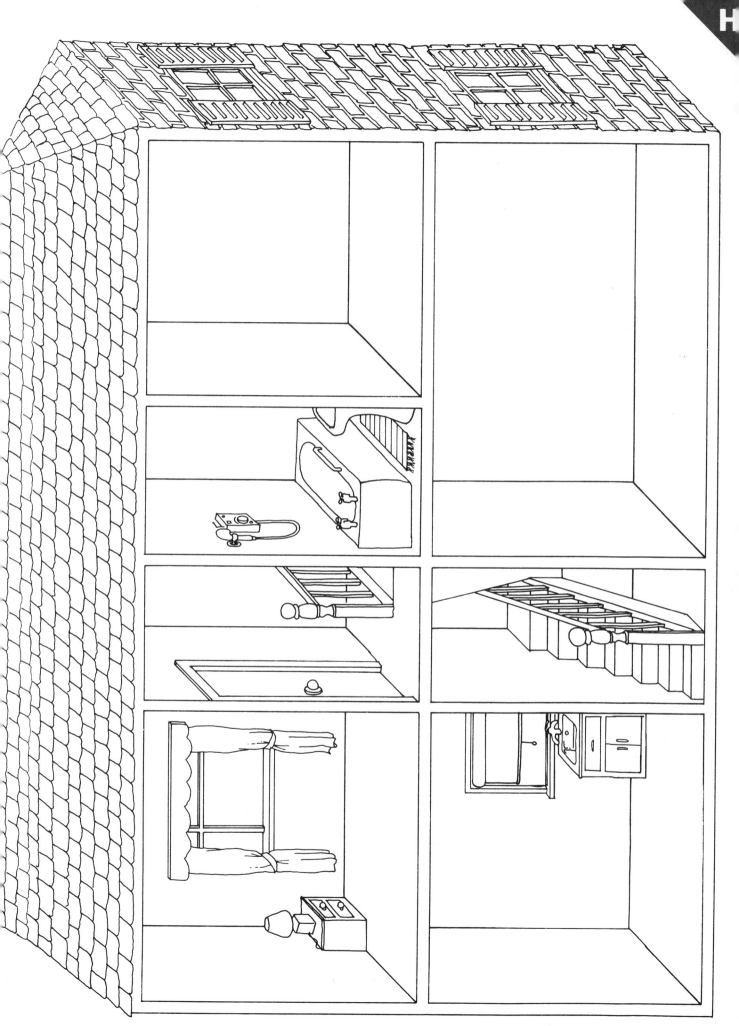

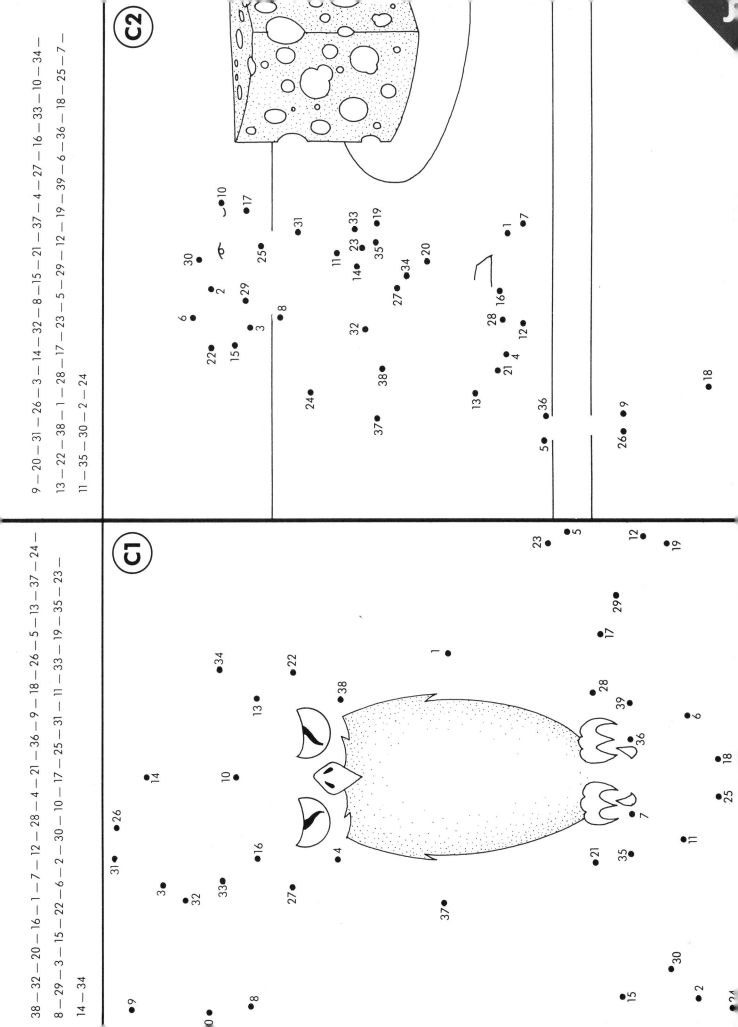

C2

9 — 20 — 31 — 26 — 3 — 14 — 32 — 8 — 15 — 21 — 37 — 4 — 27 — 16 — 33 — 10 — 34 —

13 — 22 — 38 — 1 — 28 — 17 — 23 — 5 — 29 — 12 — 19 — 39 — 6 — 36 — 18 — 25 — 7 —

11 — 35 — 30 — 2 — 24

C1

38 — 32 — 20 — 16 — 1 — 7 — 12 — 28 — 4 — 21 — 36 — 9 — 18 — 26 — 5 — 13 — 37 — 24 —

8 — 29 — 3 — 15 — 22 — 6 — 2 — 30 — 10 — 17 — 25 — 31 — 11 — 33 — 19 — 35 — 23 —

14 — 34

Do you ever . . .	Yes, always	Yes, often	Yes, sometimes	No, never
1 . . . have a party on your birthday?				
2 . . . do your homework?				
3 . . . help at home?				
4 . . . sing in the bathroom?				
5 . . . play jokes?				
6 . . . talk to animals?				

Now write about your friend.

I asked _____ .

1 He/She _____ has a party on _____ birthday.
2 _____ _____ does _____ homework.
3 _____ _____ helps at home.
4 _____ _____ sings in the bathroom.
5 _____ _____ plays jokes.
6 _____ _____ talks to animals.

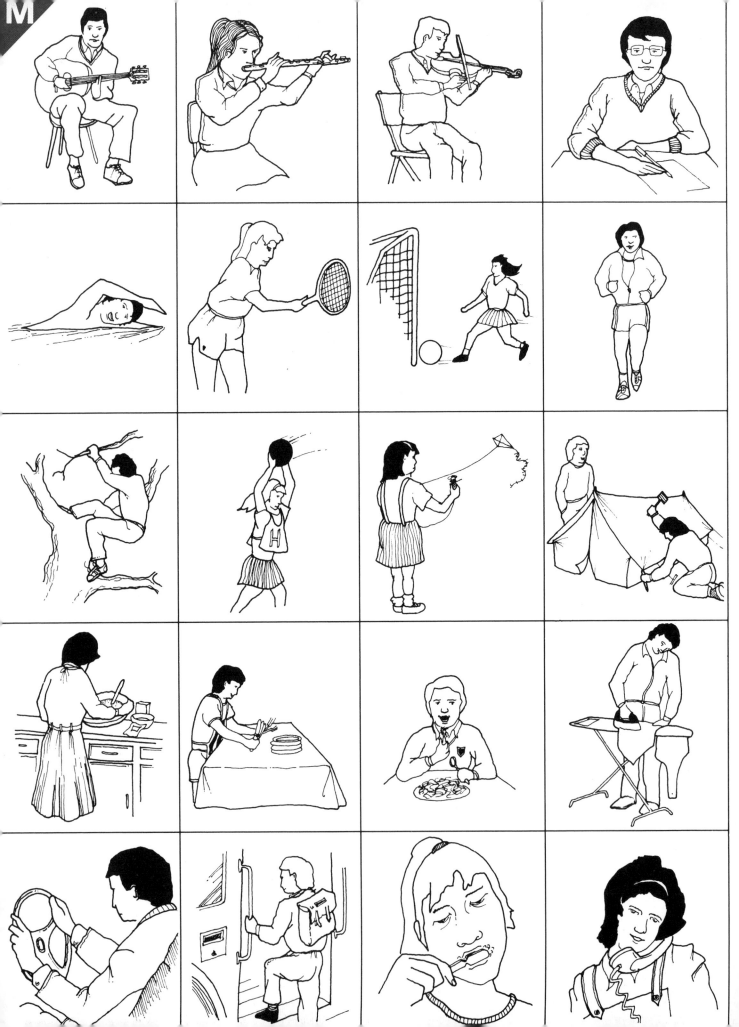

swim suit

trunks

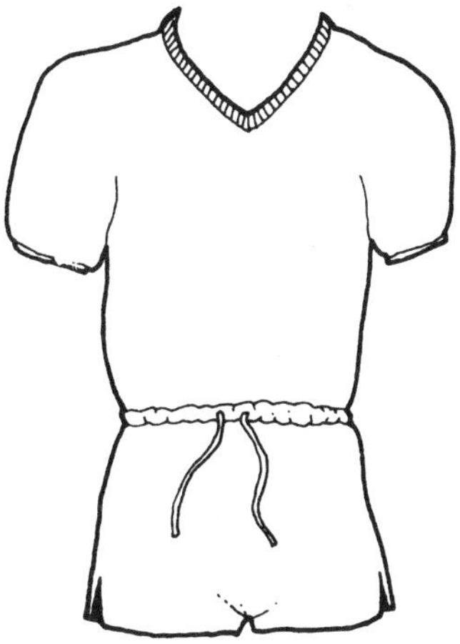

a nightdress

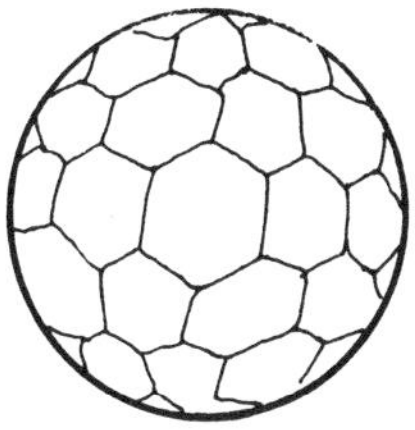

pyjamas

a football kit

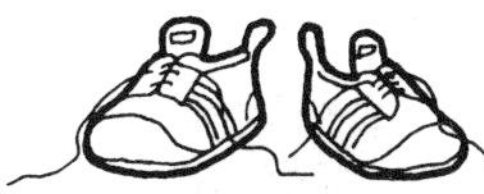

a party dress

a towel

a ball

a bag

a dance dress

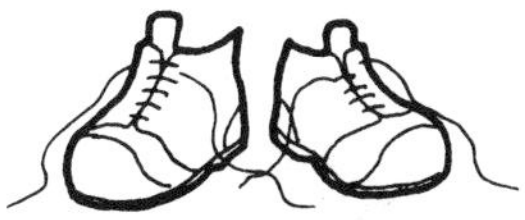

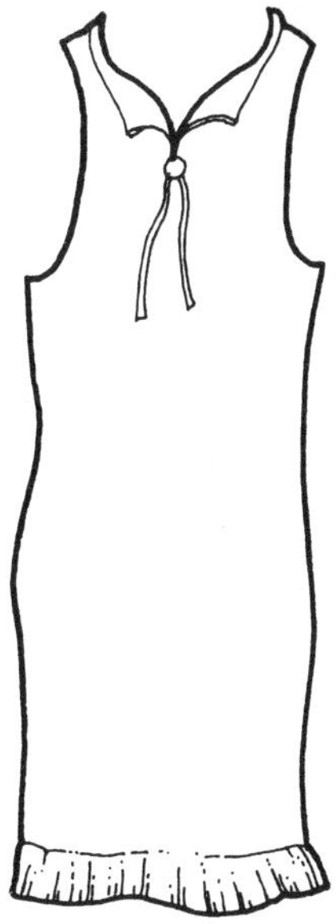

a tennis racquet

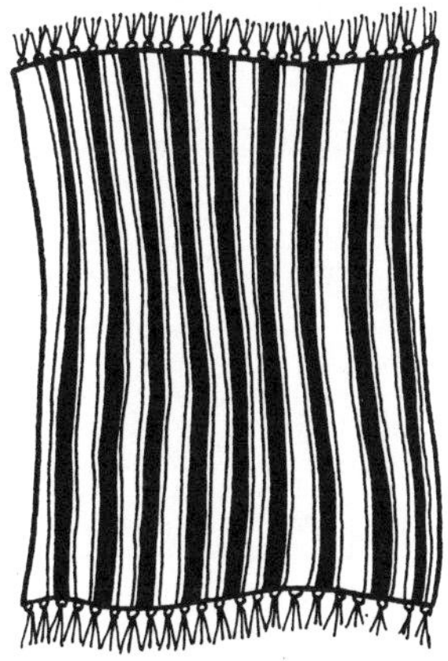

a tie

an umbrella

a present

sunglasses

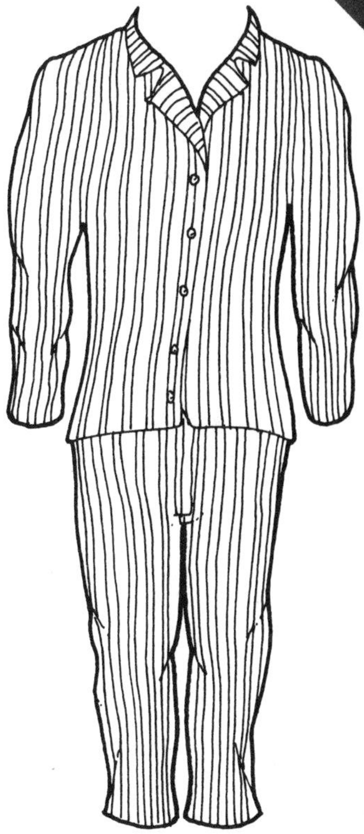

trainers

boots

slippers

dance shoes

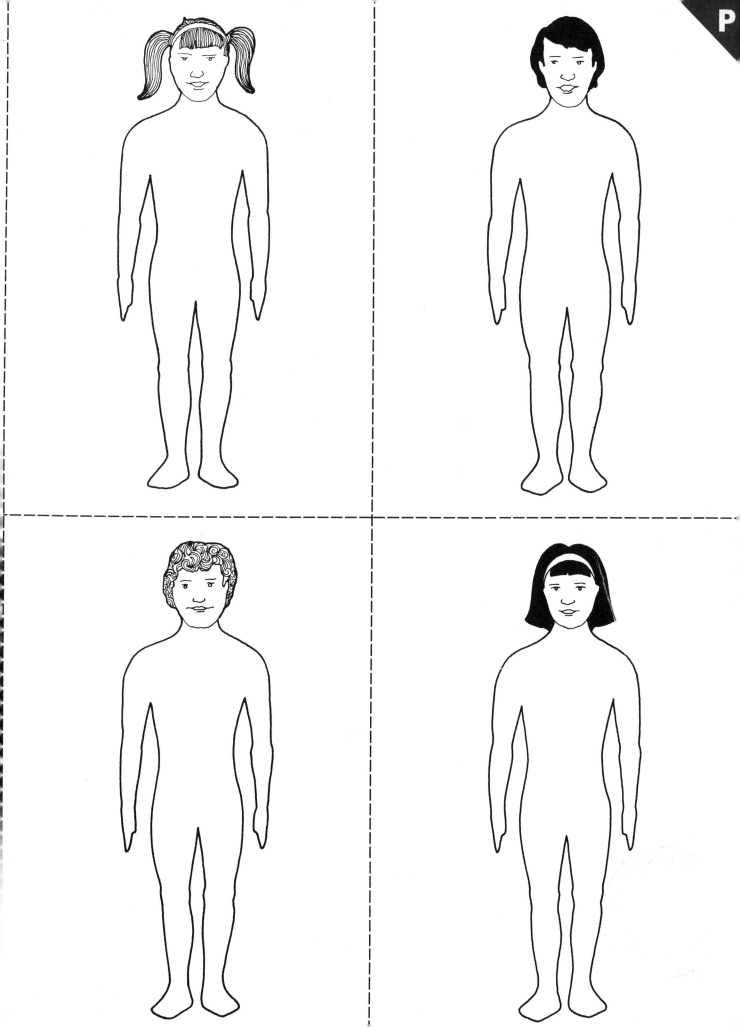

Q

Question _____

Name	Answer

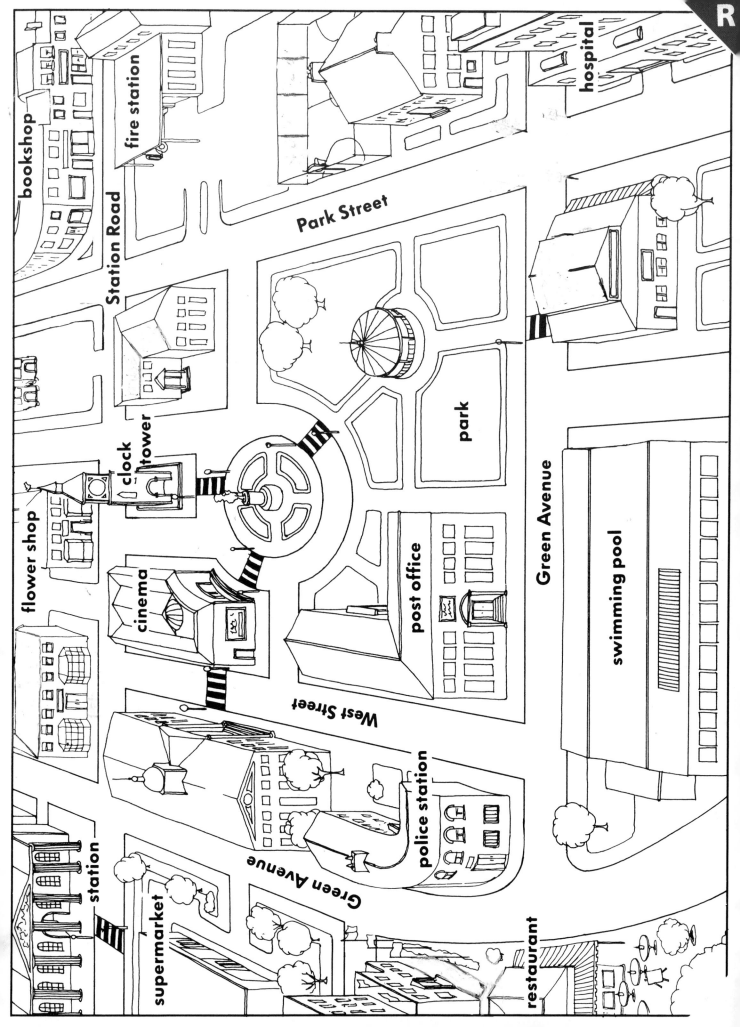

TOY BOX

AaBd

PICTURE BOOK

teddy · clocks · potato · boats · tree · jellies · box · tomatoes

Strawberries · apple · buses · watch · snakes · butterfly · dishes · train

trees · tomato · trains · boat · teddies · bus · potatoes · snake

clock · butterflies · jelly · watches · dish · apples · Strawberry · boxes

tree · train · teddy · potato · clock · boat · jelly · tomato

butterfly · watch · apple · box · Strawberry · bus · snake · dish

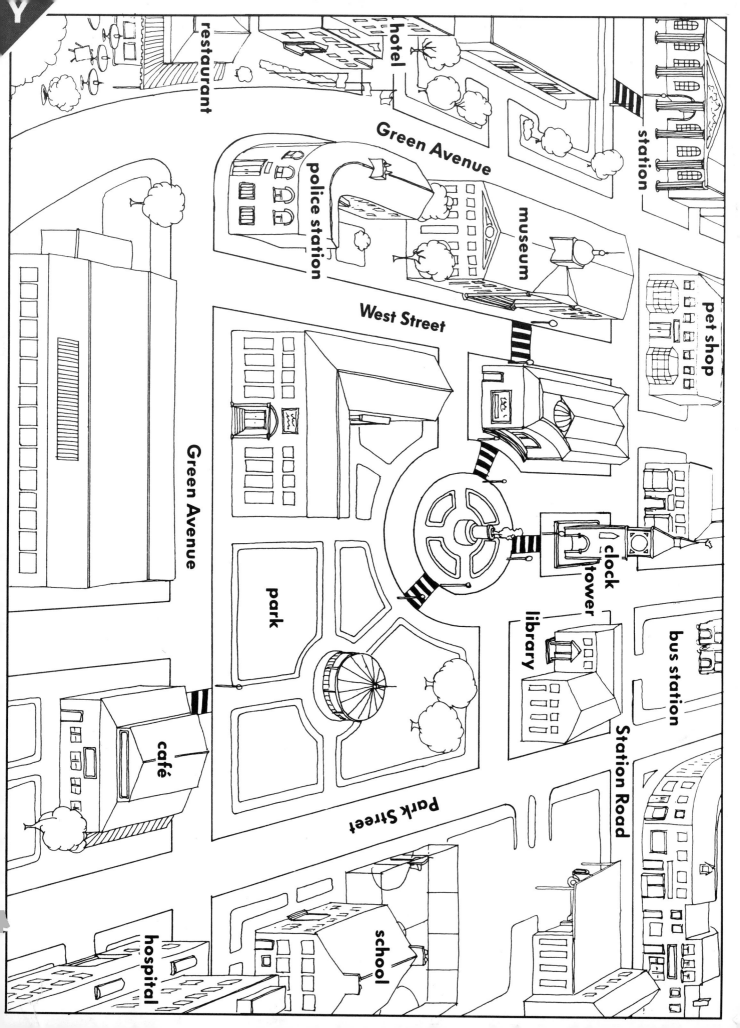

Index

Language/Function	Activities	Pages used
left, right	C6, D12, F8	R, Y
less than	F9	Q
Let's . . .	D9	
letters of the alphabet	A1, H2, H5	X
like (I'd like)	D3a	E, C, N, U, B
like (is/isn't like)	A6	H, F
like . . . best	F9a	Q
like . . . better than . . .	H10	E
likes (and dislikes)	F9a/c, F10c	Q
locations	D11	R, Y
made of	F10b, F10d, F10e	U
matching (2 types of information)	A3, A3b, A4, C2c, C9, E2, H3	C, (N), P, A, Z, T, V, K
mathematical language	F9, F10, H12	Q, A, Z, X
measuring	F9	Q
mistakes	F11	
modal verbs	B2, D3, D8, D10a, H11	Z, E, C, N, U, S, V
money	D3, F4	E, C, N, U, B
more than, less than	F9	Q
more, most	F9	Q
multiplication	H12, H12b	X
must	H11	X
My name is . . .	D1	
names	D1	
needs/doesn't need	A8	C, N
new words (revision)	C2	
noises (describing)	F15	
numbers	A1, A2, C1, G8, H11, H12	X, J
occupations	C5	O
opinions	D10	
parts of the body	C7, G5	
past continuous tense	D4	A, Z
past simple tense	A8c, D4, D6, D7, D9b, F9b	C, N, Z, A, P, M, Q
pets	D3	A, Z
phonetic sounds and spelling	B1	
places in town	D11, D12, F2b, F8	R, Y
plans	A9, D3b, D9a	P, N, E, C, N, U, A, Z
plural endings	H9	W
possessives	C7, F9c, G9	L
possibility	B2	Z
prediction	B5	
prefer	H10	E
prepositions	A6, D5, D11, F1, F2, F7, F8, H13	H, F, R, Y, T
present continuous for future	A9, D9	P, N
present continuous for present action	A7, A9, C5a, D8, D10, H16	P, N, M, S, V
present simple tense	C4, C5, C9, D2, D6, D7, F3, F9c, G9, H13	O, P, M, I, L
problem-solving	B2	Z
pronouns (personal)	F9c, G9	L
pronunciation and spelling	C2a, C2b	
questions	A3a, A9, B5, C5, C9, D2, D3a, D12a, F2, F8a, F10d, H2, H6	C, N, P, L, O, E, U, A Z, R, Y, H, T, F, G
can (and modals)	B2, D3, D12a, F4, G7	Z, A, E, C, N, U, R, Y, B
Do/Does	C5, C9	O
did	C3, F9b	Q
future tense	F9c	Q
How	D3a, F9, G6, H14	E, C, N, U, A, Z, Q
present continuous	A7, C5a, D10	M, V
present simple	C5, C9, D2, F3	O, I
Wh-questions	D2	
What	A1, A7, A9, C1b, C3, C4a, D2, D5, D10, F3, F4, F9a/b/c, F11, G7, H12	X, C, N, P, H, F, A, Z, V, I, B, Q
When	C4a, F3	I
Where	A9, D11, H11a	N, P, R, Y, X
Which	D2, F9a	Q
Who	C3, C4, G2, H13	
Why	D9	
Yes/No questions	C5, C9, F7	O, H, F

Language/Function	Activities	Pages used
revision (general)	H6	G
rhythm	C8, G1, G2, G3	
road vocabulary	D10, F2a	V
rooms	A6, D5	H, F
-s, -es, -ies plural endings	H9	W
sequencing of events	D8, D9a	S
sets	F10	
shall	G7	
shopping items	D3, F4	E, C, N, U, A, Z, B
short answers	C5, C9, F7	O, H, F
should, shouldn't	B2, D10a, G7	Z, V
sounds	F15	
sound discrimination	C2b	
spacecraft	H5	X
spelling	B1, C2, D3, E2, E3, E4, E5, E6, H1, H15, H16	E, C, N, U, A, Z, T, V, X
story-telling	B7, D6, D7, D8, D9b, F11a	P, M, S
story-writing	D7, D8, D9b	M, S
street vocabulary	D10, F2a	V
stress	C8, G1, G2, G3	
suggestions	D9	
superlatives	F9, F13a, F14a, H10	E
Suppose . . .	H11a	G
telling the time	C4, F3	I
time	C4, F3, G9	I
time phrases	D8, D9a, F3, G9	I
to (for purpose)	D9	
too	A8	C, N
touch (describing)	F12	
town facilities	D11, D12, F8	R, Y
toys	E2a, F1, F2	T
vehicles	D10, E2b, F2a	V
verbs of action	D7, D9a, E3, E5, F3, G5, G9	M
verbs of movement	C6, C7, D10, E3, E5	V, X
verbs of sound	F15	
vocabulary – *see* words		
want/don't want	D8	S
when clauses	A8c	
will for future plans	D9a, F9c	Q
word association	E8, G1	
word groups		
grammar	E3, E5, F3	
vocabulary	A3, A4, A5, A6, A8, A9, B2, C5, C7, C9, D3, D4, D5, D10, D11, D12, E2, E3, E5, E8, F1, F10, F12, F13, F14, F15, G6, G7, G10, H4, H8, H10	A, B, C, E, F, M, N, O, T, U, Z
words		
general vocabulary practice	C2, C3, E4, E6, E7, F5, F6, H1, H2, H3, H7, H15, H16	
similar in English and first language	F5	
describing sounds	F15	
with same/similar sounds	C2b, C2c	
with similar spellings	C2a, C2c	
writing stories	D7, D8, D9b	
zoo animals	B2, C9, D4, E2, E3, E5, F10, G4, G10	Z